Receiving the Gift of the Holy Spirit

Receiving the Gift of the Holy Spirit

Rev. John H. Hampsch, C.M.F.

with
Virginia Palmer

PUBLISHING COMPANY
P.O. Box 220 • Goleta, CA 93116
(800) 647-9882 • (805) 692-0043 • Fax: (805) 967-5133
www.queenship.org

© 2003 Queenship Publishing - All Rights Reserved.

Library of Congress Number # 2003095088

Published by:
  Queenship Publishing
  P.O. Box 220
  Goleta, CA 93116
  (800) 647-9882 • (805) 692-0043 • Fax: (805) 967-5133
  www.queenship.org

Printed in the United States of America

ISBN: 1-57918-238-0

TABLE OF CONTENTS

Preface	vii
Chapter 1	
General Introduction: Who is the Holy Spirit?	1
Chapter 2	
Three Separate Spiritual Stages	5
Chapter 3	
What is The Baptism In The Holy Spirit?	15
Chapter 4	
Pentecost: The Disciples Receive the Holy Spirit	21
Chapter 5	
The Gifts of the Holy Spirit	23
Chapter 6	
"Don't I Already Have The Holy Spirit?"	27
Chapter 7	
The Need for the Baptism In the Holy Spirit	31
Chapter 8	
Baptism in the Spirit—Normative for Christians	39
Chapter 9	
Symbols of the Holy Spirit in Scripture	41
Chapter 10	
Early Church Fathers on Christian Initiation and the Baptism In The Holy Spirit	47
Chapter 11	
Reasons for the Decline in the Use of the Charisms	51
Chapter 12	
Statements of the Popes on the Charismatic Renewal and the Baptism in The Holy Spirit	55
Chapter 13	
Why You Should Pray in Tongues	63
Chapter 14	
Some Benefits of Receiving the Baptism in the Holy Spirit	69
Outline of Program for Receiving the Baptism in the Holy Spirit.	81
Bibliography	95

PREFACE

Since all bars have practically the same variety of bottles on their shelves, why are customers more attracted to bars famous for their mixed drinks? Aside from drinks served "straight up," it is the bartender's "mixing skill" that determines the popularity of the bar itself.

There is no obvious connection, of course, between alcoholic "spirits" and the Holy Spirit (you knew that, didn't you?). But an analogy can be construed, perhaps, between beverage mixtures and the mixture of various source materials that have been compiled in this book to explore the subject of the Holy Spirit as the "promised Gift of the Father" (Acts 1: 4). This little treatise is an attempt to assemble an *au courant* "mixed drink" (excuse the comparison), made up of writings by various authors on the subject of the baptism in the Spirit, which I have "fleshed out" with some of my own insights. Although the book is mostly composed of paraphrased observations from my own writings and taped lectures on this subject, the extensive quotes from other authors (see the bibliography) make it a somewhat "mixed" but not exhaustive compendium of material on "pneumatology"—the study of the Holy Spirit.

My hope and prayer is that this little tome might be helpful, when used either privately or communally, in preparing candidates for receiving the baptism in the Spirit—the sublime experience that launches one into the charismatic dimension of Christian spirituality. In that sense the book is similar to any of the several presentations generically labeled as the "Life in the Spirit Seminar." With proper guidance by a reasonably mature charismatic leader, this book, hopefully, will fill that purpose, especially for groups of candidates. Privately used, it may provide at least a helpful source of information about the "Pentecostal experience" within the charismatic renewal. May the divine personified Love that is the Holy Spirit Himself guide all readers of this manual to experience an incandescent love and an abundance of His manifold gifts.

Finally, and not insignificantly, it must be noted that if it were not for the invaluable help of Virginia Palmer, a devoted champion of the charismatic renewal and a dedicated researcher, the data for this book would never have been compiled. My debt of gratitude to her is articulated as a prayer of gratitude to the Lord for her inspired and inspiring efforts in orchestrating this endeavor.

    Rev. John H. Hampsch, C.M.F.
    Claretian Tape Ministry
    P. O. Box 19100
    Los Angeles, CA 90019-0100

CHAPTER 1

General Introduction: Who is the Holy Spirit?

Widespread ignorance about the Triune God can be described as nothing short of "abysmal." This is especially true of knowledge about the least understood Person of the Holy Trinity, the Holy Spirit.

In a Barna survey in 1997, a disappointing 61% of US residents surveyed agreed with the statement that "the Holy Spirit is a symbol of God's presence or power, but is not a living entity." Even more disheartening is the fact that this heretical opinion was held by a majority or near-majority of persons in almost every Christian denomination, including traditional mainline Protestants and evangelical Christians, and was most common among young people. The real truth, not reflected by that majority opinion, can be found in Scripture. The following facts show that the Holy Spirit is truly a Person and is also truly God:

1. The fact that the Spirit's work in the Old Testament inspired the Word of God spoken by the prophets (2 Pet 1:21);

2. The correlation of Jesus' mission with the work of the Spirit (John 16:7-14);

3. The correlation of the mission of the apostles with the work of the Spirit; (see especially 1 Pet. 1:12);

4. The episode with Ananias in Acts 5, where Peter says that Ananias, in lying to the Holy Spirit, lied not to men but to God;

5. The Trinitarian baptismal formula found in Scripture (Matt. 29:19): "in the name of the Father and of the Son, and of the Holy Spirit;"

6. The recorded activities of the Holy Spirit bespeak personhood, for instance:

He speaks (Acts 13:2);

He intercedes (Rom. 8:26);

He testifies (John 15:26);

He guides (John 16:13);

He commands (Acts 16:6,7);

He appoints (Acts 20:28);

He leads (Rom. 8:14);

He reproves and convicts of sin (John 16:8);

He seals God's promise in believers' hearts (Eph. 1:13-14);

He shapes the individual's and community's life (Rom. 8:1-17).

Thus, by Scripture we know that the Holy Spirit acts as a Person, with an intellect, emotions, and will, and can be "grieved." The Spirit generally acts in and through the Church, directly or indirectly, but always by his own choice, as affirmed by Jesus' descriptive analogy in reference to the Spirit: "The wind blows wherever it pleases" (John 3:8).

Holy Scripture refers to the Holy Spirit in different ways. Sometimes the Holy Spirit is referred to as the Advocate, the Counselor, or the Paraclete; and when we pray the profession of faith during Holy Mass we say, "We believe in the Holy Spirit, the Lord, the Giver of life."

John's tells us that "God is Love" (I John 4:8). Jesus also tells us in John's gospel, as he told the Samaritan women at the well, that "God is Spirit" (John 4:24). Besides being the third Person of the Holy Trinity, we can say that the Holy Spirit is God's Spirit of Divine Love. He is essentially the mutual flow of personified Love that exists between the Father and the Son; this is the Holy Spirit that the Father promised to pour out on all mankind to draw us into the intimacy and love of the Holy Trinity. Paul wrote to the Ro-

General Introduction: Who is the Holy Spirit?

mans that "God's Love has been poured out into our hearts through the Holy Spirit that has been given to us" (Romans 5:5). In the words of St. Augustine, "What the soul is to the body of man...the Holy Spirit is to the spiritual Body of Christ, the Church." Father McDonnell writes, "...the Holy Spirit was sent on the day of Pentecost in order that he might forever sanctify the Church, and thus all believers would have access to the Father through Christ in the one Spirit" (Open the Windows, pp.6,7). And we could say that, as the oxygen in the air that we breathe provides continual health of our body, the Breath of God, the Holy Spirit, provides perpetual spiritual life for the Church.

When Jesus appeared to the apostles after his resurrection, Scripture says that "Jesus breathed on them and said "receive the Holy Spirit"—that is, the Holy Breath of Life for the Church. Paul reminded the Corinthians, "You are the temple of the Holy Spirit; God (the Trinity) dwells in you" (1 Cor. 6:19). We also recall the Church's prayer to the Holy Spirit: "Come Holy Spirit, fill the hearts of the faithful; enkindle in them the fire of your divine Love..." So, when Jesus told the disciples to "wait here and pray for the Promise of the Father," for nine days, between Ascension Thursday and Pentecost Sunday, they prayerfully prepared in the Upper Room for the infilling of that Holy Spirit's divine power and love. They made, as it were, the first "Life in the Spirit Seminar." (From this "first novena" to the Holy Spirit was derived the Catholic custom of praying novenas—nine days of prayer.)

Receiving the Gift of the Holy Spirit

CHAPTER 2

Three Separate Spiritual Stages

In my book, *What Makes a Person Charismatic?*, I explain the three basic but separate stages of spiritual growth:

1) That of the water-baptized person in the state of grace;

2) That of a "born again" Christian in an intimate relationship with Jesus;

3) That of a charismatic Christian who has received the baptism in the Holy Spirit and who maintains and cultivates that transcendent state of empowerment.

The water baptism stage is like an infant stage of Christianity that needs to grow and develop into the fullness of Christian spirituality. This process is a gradual spiritual transformation that will allow the Holy Spirit to teach, to guide and transform our lives into the likeness of Jesus. It may be compared it to a "rose bud stage" of spirituality waiting to bloom; to open up, to unfold from the "indwelling stage" (*inhabitatio*) into deeper stages of spiritual growth— the "born-again" stage (*metanoia*)—experiencing a meaningful, personal and spiritual relationship with Jesus. This, in turn is intended to prepare us to yearn for the highest "infilling stage" (*infusio*) of the Spirit—when that personal relationship with the Lord develops into an even deeper personal, intimate and empowering relationship with the Lord that endues the person with special powers of the Holy Spirit (charismatic gifts). By this empowerment we can become true evangelizers— that is, as Jesus said, "effective witnesses" (Luke 24:48 and Acts 1:8).

The "rose bud" should be encouraged to foliate ultimately into a "rose bloom"—a level of love, courageous faith and wonderworking zeal, such as the disciples experienced at Pentecost (see Acts 4:29). This is given to those who "set their mind" to seeking the fullness of the Spirit's outpouring: "Those who set their minds on the Spirit set their minds on the things of the Spirit" (Rom. 8:5). Jesus says it is given to those who "earnestly seek the Spirit" (Luke 11:13)—those who allow themselves to be "led by the Spirit of God" (Rom. 8:14). In the words of Pope John Paul II, "The Spirit is not to be grieved; the movement of the Spirit is not to be quenched, and Christians are to be led by the Spirit"; (*Open the Windows*, p. 28).

First Stage - The Water-Baptized Christian

In the first stage, through the sacrament of baptism by water, we become a Christian and open to the grace of salvation (Mark 16:16). By baptism, we are:

1) Cleansed of original sin (but not all of its effects, like illness and death).

2) Given a new birth into the life of sanctifying grace.

3) Gifted with the indwelling of the Divine Trinity, with a special emphasis on the indwelling of God's sanctifying personality, the Holy Spirit. This "indwelling of the Holy Spirit" is a doctrine affirmed by Paul: "Do you not know that you are temples of the Holy Spirit and that God dwells in you?" (1 Cor. 3:16).

4) Incorporated into the Mystical Body of Christ, the Church. In Paul's words, "In one Spirit we were all baptized into one Body...and were made to drink of one Spirit" (1 Cor. 12:12).

5) Adopted as "children of God and heirs of heaven." St. Paul writes, "You have not received the spirit of bondage again in fear; but you have received the spirit of adoption...whereby we cry, Abba, Father. It is that very Spirit bearing witness with our spirit that we are children of God...and joint heirs with Christ" (Rom. 8:15). As children we first learn to crawl; as we grow and develop in our spiritual relationship with the Holy Spirit and allow ourselves to be led by the Holy Spirit we begin to walk with Jesus more confidently and become more sensitive to the inspirations and the outpouring of the Holy Spirit into our lives.

Second Stage - The Born-Again Christian

In one sense—a rather traditional sense—it is true to say that every baptized person, even an infant, is spiritually "born again," or as Jesus said, "born of the Spirit" (John 3: 8). This is obviously a state beyond mere physical birth. But the sense in which I am using the phrase "born again" carries a further connotation—one that the Greek Fathers of the Church called "metanoia"—a word derived from the Greek verb *"metanoeo,"* which means "to think differently." 18th century French theologians referred to it as a "second conversion," by which a person experiences a new and deeper loving relationship with God through Christ.

By means of water baptism as infants, we become Christians, but not fully Christian. St. Thomas Aquinas explained that infant baptism is "valid, but not fruitful"; that is, it is incomplete in some way. Why? Because Jesus said that "he who believes and is baptized will be saved" (Mark 16:16). And St. John writes: "To all who received him, to those who believe in his name, he gave the right to become children of God...born of God" (John 1:12-13). At baptism an infant is unable to make such acts of faith in Jesus as one's Savior; hence the faith commitment must be supplied later, ideally as soon as the child reaches "the age of reason." The child should be led, by a simple educative process, to make such an act of faith-commitment in Jesus as the Redeemer who died to save each one of us individually, not just communally (see Gal. 2:20).

Repentance is that which assures that redemption is received as "salvation." Teaching this simple loving "openness to Jesus" is an obligation incumbent on the child's parents, or in their neglect, on the godparents. The "born again" assignation that relates a person to Jesus as his or her personal Savior is a human act potentiated by the Holy Spirit, as Paul explains: "It is God who makes us stand firm in Christ. He anointed us, set his seal of ownership on us, and put his Spirit in our hearts as a deposit, guaranteeing what is to come" (2 Cor. 1:21-21).

Thus, the "born-again" child or adult Christian experiences an inner "conversion" to a greater or lesser degree, as the Holy Spirit draws the person into a deeper personal relationship with Jesus.

This is the essence of the "metanoia" experience. The Christian who is "born-again" in this sense comes to know the person of Jesus Christ and has made a personal and total commitment to him as his or her personal Savior (Redeemer) and Lord (with control or lordship) over one's entire being, possessions, talents, etc. In the words of St. Paul, "I live by faith in the Son of God who loved me and gave himself for me" (Gal. 2:20).

In Scripture, the word to "know" does not mean only intellectual or cerebral knowledge; it usually implies experiential knowledge. Thus, knowing about Jesus is quite different from the more intimate state of knowing him. Scripturally, to "know" Jesus is to have a personal, heart-to-heart experience of a childlike familiarity with him. There is "an increased awareness of the ...nearness of Jesus...and that Jesus is a real person here and now in their life" (Toward A New Pentecost For A New Evangelization, p. 28).

There are various degrees in the born-again experience. For some, it is a very radical inner conversion and, sometimes a sudden spurt of spiritual growth in their life, especially when the second and third stages are reached simultaneously. Father McDonnell writes: "To receive the Spirit is to change; the experience of the power of the Holy Spirit effects a radical inner conversion and deep transformation in the lives of many" (*Toward a New Pentecost and New Evangelization*, p. 1).

1) This action of the Holy Spirit in them affects them so deeply that often years later they remember the date and the circumstances as though it were yesterday (Tape: *The Touch of The Spirit*).

2) More commonly, the born-again person develops somewhat gradually in a personal relationship with Jesus (Tape: *Touch of the Spirit*).

3) The born-again person begins to have a more meaningful grasp of the words of Jesus, "I do not call you servants...I call you friends because I have made known to you everything that I have heard from my Father" (1 John 3:9) (Tape: *The Touch of the Spirit*).

4) In this state the lure of sin and the "occasions of sin" tend to fade. No longer do deep-rooted habits of sin thrive. John writes, "Those born of God do not sin" (1 John 3:9). "Whoever has left the darkness of sin yearns for God" (Ps. 63:2-8) (*Tape: Touch of the Spirit*).

5) Because of human weakness, the person will still have failures, will still offend God. "Though the just man falls seven times a day, he will rise again" (Prov. 24:16). The greater the bondage of sin, the greater is the demonstration of God's mercy and the Holy Spirit's love.

6) The person begins to have a more sensitive conscience and have a reverent fear (dread) of offending God, more out of love for God than fear of punishment. This often misunderstood "fear of the Lord" is one of the seven sanctifying gifts of the Holy Spirit (Is. 11:2-3) (Tape: *The Touch of the Spirit*).

7) Ideally, before receiving the baptism in the Holy Spirit a person should undergo the born-again experience of repentance, of believing in, accepting and committing one's self to Jesus as his or her personal Lord and Savior. This normal sequence is stated by Paul: "When the loving kindness of our Savior appeared, he saved us...through the water of rebirth and renewal of the Holy Spirit" (Titus 3:4). "In sincerely accepting Jesus as one's personal Lord and Redeemer, one implicitly accepts the grace of salvation" (Tape: *The Touch of the Spirit*).

Having attained this second level of the "born-again" experience, receiving the baptism in the Holy Spirit brings one into the third level or charismatic stage of Christian spirituality. (It should be noted that, in some exceptional situations, the second and third stages are reached simultaneously.)

Third Stage - The Charismatic Christian

1) The Charismatic Christian is one who has been baptized into the Holy Spirit and thus launched into the experience of the infilling, not just indwelling, of the Holy Spirit, along with a

(relative) fullness of the Christian life. "I have come that they may have life, and have it to the full" (John 10:10). This experience is separate from, and usually follows, an inner conversion ("born-again") experience (see Titus 3:4); (*What Makes a Person Charismatic?*, p. 1).

2) "Water baptism makes us children of God in a special way, grafting us into the body of Christ (Gal. 3:27), while Spirit baptism gives us the charismatic power for building up that Body of Christ by becoming influential evangelizers, i.e., "effective witnesses" (Acts 1:8; Luke 24: 48-49).

3) The baptism into the Holy Spirit "is clearly distinct from and beyond the experience of becoming a Christian by being baptized into Christ (Rom.6:3) by water baptism. The two baptisms (plural—see Heb. 6:2) have totally different purposes" (*What Makes A Person Charismatic?* p. 2)

4) Paul's baptism in the Holy Spirit at the hands of Ananias came three days after his conversion on the road to Damascus, and just before his water baptism (Acts 9:3-18). Though this sequence is unusual, clearly it shows that Spirit baptism is obviously distinct from the "born again" (conversion) experience, and also distinct from water baptism.

5) The Charismatic person experiences the process of the awakening, the infilling and the release of the presence and power of the gifts and fruits of the Holy Spirit already present "inchoatively" in us through the sacraments of Baptism and Confirmation. It completes the "born-again" experience and is the beginning of the fullness of Christian spirituality. (Tape: *The Touch of the Spirit*). It adds to the "indwelling" of the Spirit a new kind of presence; an "infilling" that is meant to produce empowerment and growth—a growth in the fruits of the Spirit (Gal.5:22-23) as well as the gifts of the Spirit (1Tim.4:14; 2 Tim.1:6).

6) To prevent a kind of arrogant "charismatic triumphalism," it should be kept in mind that it is quite possible that a non-charismatic can become much holier than a charismatic, with greater

spiritual maturity and gifts of contemplative and even mystical prayer. However, to attain such holiness will be much more arduous for the non-charismatic than for the charismatic making the same effort to grow holy. Normally—that is, with all things being equal—the charismatic person can grow in the life of prayer more easily than the non-charismatic, even though the attainment of holiness of the non-charismatic, with more effort, can outstrip that of the charismatic.

In the gospel of John we read that Jesus told the disciples, "The Holy Spirit...lives with you" NOW (John 14:16)—that is, through water Baptism. "This is the Spirit of Truth, whom the world cannot receive, because it does not see (recognize) him, nor know (or experience) him; but you shall know him because he shall abide with you and shall be in you" (John 14:17); that is, on Pentecost. Thus we see that Jesus clearly distinguished between two different levels of intimacy by which the Holy Spirit can relate to an individual (*What Makes a Person Charismatic?*, p. 3). Jesus was saying, in effect, "You have one level of intimacy with the Holy Spirit now through water baptism, but you do not yet have that degree of intimacy of that infilling power of the Holy Spirit in you that will prepare you to be more effective witnesses or evangelizers in spreading the gospel" (Tape: *The Touch of the Spirit*).

When we received the sacrament of Baptism, the Holy Spirit came to dwell or to live in us by "...putting his seal on us and giving us his Spirit in our hearts as a first installment" (2 Cor.1:22). This "rose bud" stage, this "infant" stage of Christian spirituality, to become complete, needs to become a "rose bloom." By exercising our faith and expectancy, this Spirit power within us can open up to the full bloom of a truly Spirit-filled person (Tape: *The Touch of the Spirit*).

"Jesus tells us, 'I came that they may have life, and have it to the full.' (John 10:10). This abundance does not mean that we must obtain another rose; it's the same rose that is merely expanded from a bud to a bloom." (Tape: *The Touch of the Spirit*). We do not receive a second baptism. It is the same Holy Spirit that we received in the sacrament of Baptism, but now more "released" within us.

As we open ourselves to the transforming work that the Holy

Spirit wants to do in us, we move from the "rose bud" stage of our spiritual relationship with Jesus into the "rose bloom" stage of the infilling of the Holy Spirit and the "experience of the Divine hug"— to use the phrase of Pope Paul VI. This infilling of the Holy Spirit is not given in place of, but is added to, the Spirit's indwelling stage received at our water Baptism, to bring about the fullness of our love relationship with the God of love (Tape: *The Touch of the Spirit*). In the prayer of St. Paul, "I pray that you may...know (experience) the love of Christ that surpasses knowledge, that you may be filled with the love of God" (Eph.3:18).

How can we understand that which surpasses human knowledge? Paul says, "I pray that you may have power..."—that is, that power of infused knowledge that can come only from the Holy Spirit. He writes, "In every way you have been enriched in him (Jesus), in speech and knowledge of every kind so that you are not lacking in any spiritual gift" (1 Cor. 1:5). Speaking of "what God has prepared for those who love him" St. Paul writes: "These things God has revealed to us through the Spirit; for the Spirit searches everything, even the depth of God...we speak of these things in words not taught by human wisdom, but taught by the Spirit interpreting spiritual things to those who are spiritual" (1 Cor.2: 9, 10, 13).

How can the graces of each of these three stages of spirituality be lost?

First, the indwelling stage is lost by mortal sin (see 1 John 5:16-17).

Second, the born-again stage is lost by the absence of an abiding ongoing commitment to Jesus as Lord (see John 15:6).

Third, the charismatic stage or infilling by the Spirit is lost by not "living by the Spirit" (see Gal.5:16-26). St. Paul writes, "Live by the Spirit...do not gratify the desires of the flesh. For what the flesh desires is opposed to the Spirit; for these are opposed to each other, to prevent you from doing what you want" (Gal.5:16-17) (*What Makes a Person Charismatic?* p. 1).

By disregarding God's will, the baptism in the Spirit can be lost, as exemplified by the case of King Saul; he disobeyed the

Three Separate Spiritual Stages

Lord and lost his charismatic and prophetic status: "The Spirit departed from Saul" (1 Sam. 16:14). The Baptism in the Holy Spirit can be lost if it is not sustained and "nourished." Don't regard it as a definitive one-time event. It is the beginning of a day-to-day process of spiritual growth, whereby we allow the Holy Spirit to teach, guide and transform our lives, so that we can experience what St. Paul did: "I live now, not I, but Christ lives in me" (Gal.2:20).

To the Ephesians, Paul wrote, "You were taught to put away your former self (natural man) and clothe yourself with the new self...that you may know the love of Christ...and may be filled with the fullness of God" (Eph. 4:24; 3:19). "To be filled with the Holy Spirit" is an ongoing process; the actual translation of Eph. 5:18 is "continue to be filled." That is, keep on being filled with the Holy Spirit (*What Makes a Person Charismatic?*). It must be a continuously overflowing vessel, not a half-filled, stagnant one, for "God's love has been poured out into our hearts through the Holy Spirit that has been given to us" (Romans 5:5). But this gift of Love must be sought for repeatedly through prayer, as the early Christians did (*Toward a New Pentecost for a New Evangelization*, p. 4).

The book of Acts tells us that in what has been called "the second Pentecost" the disciples were again filled (refilled) with the Holy Spirit. "When they (the apostles) prayed, the place in which they were gathered together was shaken, and they were all filled with the Holy Spirit and spoke the word of God with boldness" Acts 4:31). And later "while Peter was still speaking, the Holy Spirit fell on all who heard the word" (Acts 10:44). The early Christians experienced a repetition and an ongoing flow of that Spirit power.

One way we can do the same is by committing ourselves to a more personal and intimate relationship with the Holy Spirit through personal prayer, prayerful reading of Holy Scripture, the frequent reception of the sacraments and the support of a prayer group and the community at prayer meetings.

The letter to the Hebrews tells us that some of the early Christians were neglecting their prayer meetings. "Do not forsake our assembly (prayer meetings) as some are accustomed to do" (Heb.10:25). "In the early Church, an assembly is what we call today a parish. But practically everyone in the parish was charismatic and they used their gifts during prayer meetings of these assemblies. Some of these prayer meetings or assemblies became charismatic Masses as they were incorporated into the celebration of the Eucharist" (Tape: *The Touch of the Spirit*). Thus we read in the book of Acts that the early Christians "devoted themselves to the apostles' teaching (Liturgy of the Word), to the breaking of bread (Liturgy of the Eucharist) and to the prayers" (Acts 2:42). The charismatic gifts were also used routinely during certain parts of the charismatic Mass. In later centuries, by the power of the Holy Spirit many healings also occurred during the singing in tongues, especially when used in the Mass, as attested to by St. Augustine.

CHAPTER 3

What Is The Baptism In The Holy Spirit?

We read in the book of Isaiah, that God said, "I will pour out water (Holy Spirit) on the thirsty land, and streams on dry ground; I will pour my Spirit (Living Water) on your descendants and my blessing on your offspring" (Isaiah 44:3). Fathers McDonnell and Montague explain that the Baptism into the Holy Spirit "by no means signifies a second baptism." But it is the "awakening and (and release) of the original sacramental graces (and gifts) of the Holy Spirit already present in us through the sacraments of water Baptism and Confirmation" (*Fanning the Flame*, p. 9). It is the beginning of the charismatic stage of Christian spirituality and the infilling of the power of the Holy Spirit for our own sanctification and for service in the Church and in the world.

At the Vatican II Council of 1962, Pope John XXIII symbolically "threw open the windows of the Church to allow the strong Breath of God to renew the church. The Charismatic Renewal has understood itself to be one of the ways for…that strong Breath of God, the Holy Spirit, to renew the spiritual life of the Church" (*Open the Windows*, p. 5). Foretelling the pouring out of the Spirit, through the prophet Ezekiel God said, "I will sprinkle clean water (Holy Spirit) upon you… you shall be cleansed from your idols; I shall remove from your body a heart of stone; I will give you a new heart and a new spirit. I shall put my Spirit within you" (Ezek. 36:26)

The Council was a call to personal repentance, conversion and consecration; a call for spiritual renewal and total commitment to Jesus Christ as our personal Lord and Savior; a call to "throw open our hearts," as it were, to receiving the sanctifying power of the Holy Spirit and allow the Holy Spirit to teach and guide us to holiness and service in the Church and in the world.

Father McDonnell writes, "The experience of the power of

the Holy Spirit effects a radical inner conversion and a deep transformation in the lives of many. The Holy Spirit is experienced as the power to serve and witness, to preach the gospel in word and deed; to move faith and arouse faith, (and) is manifested outwardly in ministries to the Church and the world" (*Toward a New Pentecost for a New Evangelization,* p. 1).

Among other terms, the Baptism in the Holy Spirit has also been called "the release of the Spirit" and the "renewal of the Spirit." The term, the Baptism in the Holy Spirit has been commonly accepted within the Charismatic Renewal. In the gospel of John, the evangelist, John the Baptist characterizes Jesus' ministry as that of one "who baptizes in the Holy Spirit" (John 1:33). In this sense, the term, "baptism in the Holy Spirit" has scriptural support. When Paul laid hands on them (the Ephesians) they received the Holy Spirit and spoke in tongues and prophesied" (Acts 19:2, 6). Here we see the awakening of those sacramental graces and gifts that the Ephesians had already received through water baptism.

The baptism into the Holy Spirit is the very center of the Charismatic Renewal. All four gospels speak of this Spirit baptism and tell us that Jesus is the one who baptizes us into the Holy Spirit. In the gospel of Matthew, we read "I (John, the Baptist) baptize you with water for repentance, but he, (Jesus) will baptize you with water and with fire" (Luke 3:16). The gospel of Mark reads, "…but he (Jesus) will baptize you with the Holy Spirit" (Mark 1:8).

Referring to John the Baptist, Luke's gospel reads, "I baptize you with water; but there shall come one mightier than I; he [Jesus] shall baptize you with the Holy Spirit and with fire" (Luke 3:16). John's gospel reads, "He on whom you see the Spirit descending, and remaining upon him, he it is who baptizes with the Holy Spirit" (John 1:33).

Pope Paul VI explained that the essence of the baptism into the Holy Spirit is "the experience of the Divine Hug." "Through the Baptism in the Holy Spirit, Jesus immerses us, dips us, as it were, into the Holy Spirit, who is the 'crossfire' of love between the Father and the Son, that is, into the Heart of the Holy Trinity. This is an awesome experience, to be immersed into that flow of God's Spirit of infinite Love between the Father and the Son. Paul prays that we 'may experience what is the breadth and length and height and depth...of the Love of Christ that surpasses knowledge; that you may be filled with the Love of God' (Eph.3:18); he prays that we may experience and 'taste' who God is and 'see' him with the eyes of our heart" (Tape, *The Touch of the Spirit*).

Each person may experience the touch of the Holy Spirit in a different way. Some of the visible signs of the touch of the Spirit occasionally include crying or laughing or resting in the Spirit; and at the same time, some candidates may feel a deeper sense of God's presence or a deep sense of repentance or joy or peace or a sensation of warmth in the body. Still others may feel nothing at all until later. They may also experience a definite and unforgettable change of heart. They may become so touched by God's Spirit that they always remember the day they said "Yes" to God and experienced the power of the Holy Spirit in their life. (Tape: *The Touch of the Spirit*). This change of heart, this personal "experience of the power of the Spirit leads not only to a realization that Jesus is real and present, but also leads to new kind of hunger: hunger for prayer, most especially the prayer of praise; (and) hunger for the Word of God...a profound sense of the presence of God... a move toward community, new depth of personal relationships, greater appreciation and respect of the sacramental life, of the teaching authority of the Church and the experience of the gifts of the Holy Spirit" (*Toward a New Pentecost*, p. 63).

In his address to the 2nd International Leader's Conference, Pope Paul VI explained that "the Spirit (of God) introduces the believer into the flow of love by which the Father loves the Son in the Holy Spirit" (*Open the Windows*, p. 11).

This experience brings us into a deeper and more personal relationship with a God of love and in the charismatic dimension of Christian spirituality. Through this Spirit baptism, we begin to become more aware of and experience the beginning of the infilling presence and love of the Holy Spirit. The more we grow in the love of God, the more of the God of love we want; and the more we desire to reach out and share that love for the healing of the brokenness and woundedness of others.

With the baptism in the Spirit, we experience the release of some of the nine "classical" charismatic gifts of the Holy Spirit that Saint Paul refers to in chapter 12 of 1 Corinthians, such as the gifts of tongues, healing, faith, etc.

One of the most important developments in the Renewal is the move toward community where "clergy and laity alike share their lives and stand in contrast to individualism today" (*Toward a New Pentecost and a New Evangelization* p. 60). In October, 1973, speaking to the 1st International Leaders Conference, Pope Paul VI said, "The invigorating breath of the Holy Spirit has come to awaken slumbering energies in the Church; to arouse, to awaken sleeping charisms (gifts of the Holy Spirit)" (*Open the windows*, p. 3). "Do not quench the Spirit," says Paul, "but fan into flame the gift of God that is within you through the laying on of hands" (1 Thess. 5:19; 2 Tim.1:6).

In our intimate love relationship with God, we can better understand what Paul wrote to the Romans: "The charity of God is poured forth in our hearts by the Holy Spirit who is given to us" (Romans 5:5); that same Holy Spirit and Fire of Love had by our Blessed Mother Mary and the disciples on the first Pentecost.

The Baptism into the Holy Spirit is a personal religious experience and a total commitment to Jesus in which the person experiences the presence and love of the Holy Spirit and the release of that untapped power of the gifts of the Holy Spirit already present in us through water baptism. It is a personal rededication and renewal of our baptismal promises and the riches of our faith.

1) It is a personal experience because it is an experience only between the soul and the Holy Spirit. When we received the sacrament of Baptism, the Holy Spirit brought us into the Mystical Body of Christ, the Church. Through the Baptism in the Holy Spirit, Jesus immerses us deeper into God's Holy Spirit of love. We experience the "divine hug," the personal embrace of God's love as a personal Pentecost. Paul says, "You have been given the spirit of adoption whereby you cry Abba, Father. It is that very Spirit bearing witness to our spirit that we are children...heirs of God and joint heirs with Christ" (Rom. 8:15-16).

2) It is a personal commitment because each person makes the individual decision to accept Jesus as his or her personal Lord

and Savior. We seriously and totally give to Jesus all our human experiences, our past, present and future and all our possessions for now and for eternity. In doing this, we recognize that "Jesus is Lord," to whose lordship we surrender. We see him as God's Gift to us, for "every perfect gift comes from above, coming down from the Father" (James 1:17).

3) It is a religious experience because our intellect, imagination and memory; our conscience, our will, our spirit and our body; all our human faculties are touched and changed by the action of the Holy Spirit of love who "draws and directs us to Himself," thus helping us to grow in a more intimate relationship of Love, the essence of sanctity (*Divine Intimacy*, p. 572). To experience this, we need to have a living child-like faith, openness, and a real sense of expectancy of what the Holy Spirit can do in our lives.

4) It gives us the anointing power or special supernatural ability to grow in holiness faster and to bear witness to Jesus in ways that could come only from the Holy Spirit. "In the Council of Jerusalem, one of the early Fathers of the Church explained that the Spirit is a new kind of water. What the Spirit touches, the Spirit changes. The Spirit sanctifies the Christian, transforming the baptized into the likeness of Christ" (*Fanning the Flame*, p. 18).

The prophet Joel, quoted in Acts 2:17, tells us that "God said, 'I will pour out my Spirit, (my Living Water), on all mankind.'" Let us imagine ourselves as a sponge in a container of water. The purpose of the sponge is to soak up, to absorb and to have all the areas of the sponge become saturated with the surrounding water. To an extent, the nature of the sponge is changed and is prepared for use.

Let us ask ourselves, do we really want the Holy Spirit, God's Living Water, to saturate, to fill all the areas of our being so that we can know more of the fullness of God's Spirit power and personal love for each of us? Are we really sincere when we sing, "Spirit of the Living God, fall afresh on me; melt me, mold me, fill me use me?" Do we really want that special personal anointing of the Holy

Spirit on our minds, our memory, our imagination, our conscience, our will, our emotions, our spirit, and our body? If we do, the Baptism in the Holy Spirit will be the beginning of that infilling, that saturation of the Spirit of God's love and power in our life that will help us to think like Jesus, to speak like Jesus and to act like Jesus. John's gospel tells us that "we are God's children now; what we will be has not yet been revealed. What we do know is this: when he (Jesus) shall appear, we will be like him" (1John 3:2). And as Paul wrote to the Romans, "For those whom he foreknew he also predestined to be conformed to the image of his Son (Jesus)" (Rom. 8:29), "who is the reflection of God's glory and the exact imprint of Gods very being" (Heb.1:3).

We have lived so long with old habits, old ways that we need to relearn how to recognize and follow the inspirations of the Holy Spirit in the work of our sanctification. "You were taught to put away your former (sinful) way of life, your old self...to clothe yourself with the new self, created according to the image of God in true righteousness and holiness" (Eph. 4:23-24).

As we grow in our personal relationship with God, we become more sensitive to what the Holy Spirit is trying to say to us. In his book, *Listening to God*, Father William McCarthy explains that "God speaks to us in many ways; some of those ways are through our minds and in our hearts, in our human spirits. God's normal interior way of speaking to his children is through their own thoughts, which the Spirit from within, puts into our minds. This happens so naturally most of the time that his children miss the realization that the 'insights' or thoughts that come to them, come from the Holy Spirit." (*Listening to God: Ways to Hearing God's Voice*). The Spirit thus helps us to have a deeper understanding of the gospel message and how we can apply it to our daily life.

The next interior way (that the Holy Spirit speaks) is through the impressions he makes upon our hearts. "When we realized that God has placed his Spirit within us to enlighten our minds and inflame our hearts to do his will, we begin to trust the impulses of his Holy Spirit within us," (*Listening to God*, p. 6, 7). We begin to better understand what Saint Paul wrote to the Romans: "May you have the renewal of your minds, so that you may know God's will, what is good...and acceptable ...and...perfect" (Rom. 12:2).

CHAPTER 4

Pentecost: The Disciples Receive the Holy Spirit

The historic event of Pentecost is succinctly described in the book of Acts: "When the day of Pentecost came, they were all together in one place. Suddenly a sound like the blowing of a violent wind came from heaven and filled the whole house where they were sitting. They saw what seemed to be tongues of fire that separated and came to rest on each of them. All of them were filled with the Holy Spirit and began to speak in other languages as the Spirit enabled them" (Acts 2:1-4). Prior to this event Jesus himself had experienced the gift of tongues, for in the book of Hebrews, one translation has it that "he groaned in the Spirit" (Heb.5:7). St. Paul uses that word in Romans 8:26: "The Spirit intercedes for us with groans that words cannot express."

Since Mary was present at the Pentecost event, she also was filled with the Holy Spirit and spoke in tongues, for the passage says that "all" present there received that gift. And as Mary became mother of the physical body of Christ, so again, by the power of the Holy Spirit at Pentecost, she became the Mother of the Mystical Body of Christ, the Church. Father McDonnell writes, "In the midst of the apostles was Mary, the one who accepted the Holy Spirit's greatest gift: the life of Jesus. May she who thus became the Mother of the Church be in a special way your Mother and the model of the Renewal in the Church" (*Open the Windows,* p. 48).

"When the crowd heard the disciples speaking of God's great deeds of power in their own native language, they were amazed and asked one another what does this mean?" Others said, "They are filled with new wine!" But Peter stood up and raising his voice said, "These are not drunk; it is only nine o'clock in the morning. No this is what was spoken of by the prophet Joel. 'In the last days,' God said, 'I will pour out my Spirit on all mankind'" (Acts

2:17). And to the first converts Peter explains, "The Promise of the Spirit is for you, for your children, for all who are far away, for everyone whom the Lord our God calls to him" (Acts 2:39).

"When Peter spoke to the crowd about this Jesus whom they crucified, his audience, when they heard this, were cut to the heart and asked Peter and the disciples 'What shall we do, brothers?' Peter replied, 'Repent and be baptized...in the name of Jesus Christ so that your sins may be forgiven, then you will receive the gift of the Holy Spirit'" (Acts 2:37-38). "Those who accepted the message were baptized and that day about three thousand persons were added, and day by day the Lord added to the number those who were being saved" (Acts2:41-47). "As Jesus' baptism in the Spirit (in the River Jordan) was the beginning of his pubic life, so, Pentecost, the baptism in the Spirit for the Apostles was the beginning of the evangelization of the world by the infant Church. The Spirit is given to those who proclaim the Word, as well as to those who hear it. What was true of the Church in its beginning is true also today. If there is no Spirit present, there is no evangelization." (*Open the Windows*, p. l9; "*Evangelization in the Modern World*").

"As a faith-filled community, in every gathering for a Life in the Spirit Seminar, like the Apostles, we too gather together, prayerfully preparing for the release of that same empowerment of the Holy Spirit in our lives. When we receive the Baptism in the Holy Spirit, we are not just joining another movement; we are embracing more of the fullness of Christian life in the Church" (*Fanning the Flame*, p. 22). Pope Paul VI said that he desired that the leaders see the renewal not as "a movement in the Church, but the Church itself in movement," (*Open the Windows*, p. 19).

The Baptism in the Holy Spirit is the very heart of the Charismatic Renewal and the renewal of a perpetual Pentecost of today's "Church in movement" (*Open the Windows*, p. 9; Doc. 5, *2nd Inter. Leader's Conference*, 1975). To be baptized into the Holy Spirit is to make a personal decision to allow the Holy Spirit to completely fill our minds and heart with God's love and lead us to holiness; to give over complete control of our lives to the love and guidance of the Holy Spirit in all of our human experiences. We thus are guided by the Holy Spirit in doing God's will. In this sense we are allowing the Holy Spirit to be in control of our thoughts, word and actions.

CHAPTER 5

The Gifts of the Holy Spirit

Only if we have truly grasped something of the awesome majesty and beauty of God's Holy Spirit, the Gift of Gifts, the Lord and Giver of Life, can we them approach the study of the gifts that he wants to bestow on us. A teaching on the gifts of the Holy Spirit is an extensive study by itself—and an important one. Paul tells the Corinthians in the opening of Chapter 12 of his first epistle to them, "About the spiritual gifts, brothers, I do not want you to be ignorant."

There are two sets of gifts of the Holy Spirit: First, there is the series of the seven sanctifying gifts, found in Isaiah 11:2-3, which are enhancements of the life of virtue; they are powerful means by which the Holy Spirit, the Sanctifier, sanctifies us, i.e., makes us holy. It is by these special gifts that he lifts us to higher realms of holiness if we are truly desirous to become holy with a deep spiritual zeal or yearning for our personal sanctification for God's glory. Since they are not primarily communitarian but personal, they are often referred to as the Holy Spirit's "personal" gifts.

These gifts that help to sanctify us are Wisdom, Understanding, Counsel, Fortitude, Knowledge, Piety and Fear of the Lord. (Fear of the Lord is not a fear of God's punishment, but a fear or dread of offending a loving God—a reverence or reverential "fear.") These seven gifts are greater than the charismatic gifts because they lead us to holiness. These are the gifts that we learn about in catechism class in preparing for the sacrament of Confirmation.

Those who receive the baptism into the Holy Spirit authentically will receive especially one of those "non-charismatic" gifts with it, which is the gift of Understanding. By this great gift, God's revelation, especially in Scripture, becomes very meaningful to us. By this gift we begin to understand God's Word in a more profound way" (Tape: *The Touch of the Spirit*). This gift is one of the most powerful for sanctifying us, for it immerses us in a profound appreciation of God's revelation. Pope Paul VI referred to the grace of the Renewal of the Holy Spirit as the "the experience of a new and perpetual Pentecost"; that is, a personal Pentecost for the "renewal of the spiritual life" of each member of the spiritual body of Christ, the Church—a chance for the Church and the world" (*Open the Windows*, p.10).

The other set of gifts embraces what is known as the charismatic gifts (or charisms) are designed for "the common good" of the Christian community (1 Cor. 12:7), and hence in that sense are not "personal." There are at least 25 of these charisms mentioned in the New Testament; they're found primarily, but not exclusively, in 1 Corinthians, chapters 12 and 14. These include the nine primary—or so-called "classical"—charismatic gifts that Paul lists in 1Corinthians 12:8-10, These primary charismatic gifts fall into three main categories:

1) The word gifts (the gift of prophecy, the gift of tongues, and the gift of interpretation of tongues);

2) The power gifts (the gift of faith, the gift of healing, and the gift of miracle-working);

3) The revelation gifts (the utterance of knowledge, the utterance of wisdom and discernment of Spirits). (Tape: *The Touch of the Spirit*).

Ideally, all these charismatic gifts, designed for the welfare of the Christian community, should be operative in every prayer group, but not in every person in the group, for scripture tells us that "the Spirit allots to each one individually as the Spirit chooses" (1Cor. 12:11). Experiencing the release of these gifts of the Holy Spirit is only secondary to receiving the Spirit himself; they are signs or evidence of the Spirit operating in a ministerial manner in the Church (see *A New Pentecost for a New Evangelization*, p.10).

However, one special gift of the Spirit is that of the "heavenly language"—the gift of tongues—with the four ways that St. Paul describes its use in 1 Cor. 14. This gift, which will be explained in more detail in Chapter 13 of this book, is often taken to be the primary outward sign of assurance that one has been baptized in

Pentecost: The Disciples Receive the Holy Spirit

the Holy Spirit. If you do not have the gift of tongues you cannot be sure that you have been authentically baptized in the Holy Spirit. (Tape: *The Touch of the Spirit*). In the words of Pope Paul VI, "No endowment with charisms (gifts) by themselves makes one pleasing to God. Love alone does that" (*Open the Windows,* p.11). This gift of praying in tongues is the only charismatic gift that can make us holy, because it is a form of prayer that is love-clothed, (1 Cor. 14:14). The other charismatic gifts (performing healings, etc.) do not make us holy, as the sanctifying (personal) gifts would do. The charismatic gifts in general are "power tools" that are designed to serve to build up the faith-experience in the community itself as forms of the Spirit's promised power.

An early example of the release of charismatic power was the use of the gift of prophecy which itself referred to a future and even more dynamic power release by those gifted with it. Referring to the grace of Pentecost, in Acts, chapter 2, the prophet Joel is quoted: "'In the last days,' God said, 'I will pour out my Spirit on all mankind. And your sons and daughters shall prophesy; and your young men shall see visions; your old men shall dream dreams'" (Acts 2:17). When this Spirit would be outpoured, it would not be given merely in small portions or measures. This prophecy was presented in anticipation of the coming day when the Spirit would be outpoured in all its fullness.

The book of Acts also tells us how this prophecy began to be fulfilled at the first Pentecost in Jerusalem. Before Jesus ascended into heaven, he said to the disciples, "Do not go out of Jerusalem; wait here and pray for the promise of the Father" (Acts 1:4). John [the Baptist] baptized you with water, but you will be baptized with the Holy Spirit not many days from now [on Pentecost]. You shall receive power when the Holy Spirit comes on you. You shall be witnesses for me in Jerusalem, in all Judea and Samaria, and to the ends of the earth" (1:8). Just before Jesus ascended into heaven, he told the disciples, "I am sending you what my Father promised; so stay here in the city until you are clothed with power from on High." (Luke 24:49).

Referring to the "power from on high," Jesus affirmed, "You shall receive power when the Holy Spirit comes on you" (Acts

1:8). He was saying to his disciples, and to us, that they and we are not ready yet to be effective witnesses for him through preaching the gospel. We are told to wait for that grace and power of his Spirit—"the Spirit of Truth, whom the Father will send in my name, will teach you everything and remind you of all that I have said to you" (John 14:26).

Jesus was saying, in effect, that without the charisms and grace of his Spirit, even the most convincing preparation of his word would not have the power to change or stir the hearts of men. He showed that they needed deeper faith-filled convictions, along with courageous love and boldness that only His Spirit could give to make their mission fruitful. Those power gifts would be tools to be used to evangelize—that is, to persuade others to come back to God or to come closer to God. It would empower them to become more effective witnesses by doing things beyond natural capabilities, like miraculously healing and exorcizing afflicted persons. He told them to stay in Jerusalem to await the outpouring of that Spirit with his empowerment. (Tape: *The Touch of the Spirit*).

CHAPTER 6

"Don't I Already Have The Holy Spirit?"

The question is often asked, "Didn't I receive the Holy Spirit when I was baptized?" Yes. The indwelling, but not infilling or empowerment, of the Holy Spirit begins with water Baptism.

Two principal effects of water baptism are the purification from sins and a new birth in the Spirit (*C.C.C.* p. 330). Paul asks the Corinthians, "Do you not know that you are God's temple...that God's Spirit dwells in you?" (1 Cor. 3:16).

The sacrament of Confirmation brings an increase and deepening of the baptismal grace; it gives us a special strength of the Holy Spirit to spread and defend the faith by word and action as true witnesses of Christ (*C.C.C.* p. 330).

John the Baptist had the Holy Spirit in the womb of his mother, Elizabeth. The gospel of Luke relates that John the Baptist "leaped for Joy" when Elizabeth heard Mary's voice (Luke 1:44). In traditional Catholic piety that is interpreted as having been a kind of pre-birth baptism for John. Mary, our Mother, wants to help each of us also to be filled with that same love and joy of the Holy Spirit.

Even before Pentecost, on Easter night, the disciples had received the Holy Spirit in the expression of a ministerial gift—that of being equipped to forgive sins. Because they were afraid of being persecuted or killed as followers of Jesus, they had locked themselves in the Upper Room in Jerusalem. There Jesus appeared to them and said, "As the Father has sent me...I send you." Then he breathed on them [the Holy Breath of the Spirit] and said, "Receive the Holy Spirit. If you forgive anyone his sins, they are forgiven..." (John 20:22).

Later, in the book of Acts, Jesus tells the disciples, "John [the Baptist] baptized you with water, but you will be baptized with the

Receiving the Gift of the Holy Spirit

Holy Spirit not many days from now" (Acts 1:5). That is, just before his ascension Jesus said this because he wanted the disciples to receive a special anointing, a supernatural empowerment that would prepare them for their public ministry.

Matthew's gospel tells us that "...she [Mary] was found to be with child from the Holy Spirit" (Matthew 1:18). From the first moment of his existence, Jesus was filled with the Holy Spirit. The conception of Jesus in Mary's womb by the power of the Holy Spirit marks him as the Son of God and the Messiah (*Toward a New Pentecost for a New Evangelization*, p. 6).

When Jesus was baptized in the River Jordan, he received a special anointed power in preparation for his public ministry. "God anointed Jesus of Nazareth with the Holy Spirit and with power" (Acts 10:38).

When he was baptized in the Jordan, Jesus also received the Spirit as a personal endowment, giving power and authority to fulfill his messianic mission foretold by the prophet, Isaiah, "The Spirit of the Lord is upon me, he has anointed me to bring good news to the oppressed; to heal the contrite of heart; proclaim release to captives...to comfort all who mourn" (Isaiah 61:1-2).

Through water baptism we are cleansed of original sin, become children of God, members of the spiritual Body of Christ, the church, and the Holy Trinity comes to dwell in us. For our sake, Jesus allowed John the Baptist to baptize, to wash him, in the River Jordan. "For our sake God made Him Jesus to be sin so that in Him we might become the righteous of God" (2 Cor. 5:21). Consider the implications of this as found in Matthew 3:16-17:

1) "Jesus, being baptized, came up from the water." When we receive the sacrament of water baptism, we "come up from the water" cleansed of original sin.

2) "The heavens were opened to him." Being cleansed of original sin through baptism, the gates of heaven were opened for us.

3) "He [John] saw the spirit of God descending like a dove and coming upon him." Through Baptism the Holy Spirit comes to dwell in us.

4) "And a voice from heaven said...." Because our Baptism made us members of the body of Christ, the Church, our guiding "voice from heaven" is the same Holy Spirit guiding us through our Holy Father, Church tradition, the teaching magisterium of the Church and Holy Scripture. In the words of Jesus to the apostles, "He who listens to you, listens to me, and whoever rejects you, rejects me, and whoever rejects me, rejects the one who sent me" (Luke 10:16).

5) "A voice from heaven said, 'this is my beloved Son in whom I am well pleased.'" Here the Father publicly reveals the Trinity, the mission of Jesus and who Jesus is: the voice of the Father is heard from heaven; of Jesus he says: "this is my Beloved Son in whom I am well pleased; and the Holy Spirit of God descends on Jesus in the form of dove." Through Baptism we are sealed as Christians by the Holy Spirit. St. Paul says that we have become children of God, not by nature, but that "we have... been given a Spirit of adoption whereby we [also] cry Abba, Father" (Rom.8:15).

As Jesus' baptism (in the River Jordan) was at the beginning of his public life, so Pentecost, the baptism of the Holy Spirit for the Apostles, was the beginning of the evangelization of the world by the infant Church (*Open the Windows*, p. 19). Similarly, as Jesus went down into the water, was anointed with the Holy Spirit and declared the Son of God (by the Father) so, those becoming Christian, go down into the water of baptism, are anointed, receive the Holy Spirit and are declared daughters and sons of God" (*Toward a New Pentecost for a New Evangelization*, p. 7).

CHAPTER 7

The Need for the Baptism In the Holy Spirit

In the very beginning of his public life and at the end of his public life, Jesus emphasized the need for and the difference between water baptism and the baptism into the Holy Spirit. Again, these two baptisms represent two different levels of spiritual intimacy with Jesus, and have totally different purposes. (Tape: *The Touch of the Spirit*).

In the beginning of his public life, Jesus told Nicodemus that we "must be born again of water and the Spirit, so we can experience more fully the awakening of the Holy Spirit for our inner conversion and total commitment to Jesus as our personal Lord and Savior (John 3:5); (Tape: *The Touch of the Spirit*).

So, Jesus tells us that the indwelling, the "inhabitation" of the Holy Spirit, this "infant" stage of Christian spirituality through water baptism, is not enough. We cannot stop there. He wants us to have the infilling, the fullness of the Holy Spirit; the fullness of Christian spirituality which begins with the baptism in the Holy Spirit (Tape: *The Touch of the Spirit*). When we receive the sacrament of Baptism, it is as if God had sown the "seeds" of the graces and gifts of the Holy Spirit in the "soil" of our heart. But we need to allow the Holy Spirit to clear the "soil" of our hearts of sin, loosen, cultivate and water those "seeds" so that they can open up and produce the harvest of the fruits of the Holy Spirit in our life that will help to lead us to our sanctification, be a support to the community and to equip us to witness to Christ in ways that are beyond our human capabilities.

"The fruit of the Holy Spirit is love; like the segments of one orange, the one fruit (love) has multiple expressions: joy, peace, patience, kindness, goodness, faithfulness, gentleness and self-control (Gal. 5:22-23). These segments of the fruit of the Spirit are behavior patterns that are found in the person who is truly Spirit-filled" (Tape: *The Touch of the Spirit*). Matthew's gospel reminds us, "By their fruits you will know them" (Matt. 7:16).

At the end of his public life, Jesus again speaks of the two baptisms. Just before he ascended into heaven, Jesus said to his disciples, "Do not leave Jerusalem, but wait for the gift my Father promised, which you have heard me speak about [the Holy Spirit]. John baptized you with water, but in a few days you will be baptized with the Holy Spirit.... You will receive power when the Holy Spirit comes on you, and you will be witnesses in Jerusalem...and to the ends of the earth" (Acts 1:5-8). (Tape: *The Touch of the Spirit*). What is this power? "It is a power manifesting itself in a courageous faith animated by a new love which enables one to undertake and accomplish great things beyond one's natural capabilities for the Kingdom of God" (*Toward a New Pentecost For a New Evangelization*, p. 28).

"This Spirit power that dwells within us comes to visibility in the gifts. It manifests itself in such a way that "what you see and hear is the outpouring of that Spirit" and its impact on those who see and hear" (Acts 2:23); (*For a New Pentecost and a New Evangelization*, p. 6). The Acts of the Apostles tells us that "those who heard Peter preach 'were cut to the heart'" (2:37). When one of the disciples of John the Baptist asked Jesus if he was the one who was to come...Jesus replied, "Tell John what you see and hear; the blind see, the lame walk, the lepers are cleansed, the deaf hear, the dead raised and the poor have the good news brought to them" (Matt. 11:4-5).

Father McDonnell writes, "The church today is in need of the full awareness, expectation and openness for a greater desire for that same Spirit power and more of the fullness of Christian spirituality" (*Toward a New Pentecost*) p. 23).

This power, openness and awareness include the charismatic gifts, and the right and obligation to use the gifts for our own spiritual welfare and that of the community. In the 2nd Vatican Council the Decree of the Apostolate of the Laity refers to both the right and the obligation to use these gifts, saying that "...there arises for each of the faithful, the right and the duty of exercising those gifts in the Church and in world for the good of humans and the development of the Church."

Why did the disciples need this special anointing power? Jesus was saying to them and to us, "You are not ready yet to effectively proclaim the gospel for me." No one can even say, "'Jesus is Lord,' except by the Holy Spirit" (1 Cor. 12:3). But Jesus assures the disciples that "the Holy Spirit that the Father will send in my name, will teach you everything, and remind you of all that I have said to you" (John 14:26). Jesus tells us not to go out on your own and try to be influential witnesses for him without the power of his Spirit. Make a Life In The Spirit seminar. Be baptized into the Holy Spirit. Through water baptism we become good Christians; but we need the empowerment of spirit-filled Christians, for both our personal sanctification and for fruitful service in the church and in the world. (Tape: *The Touch of the Spirit*). It was as if Jesus were again reminding his disciples and us, "I am the Vine and you are the branches; without the power of my Spirit, you cannot bear fruit that will last because apart from me you can do nothing" (see John 15:5).

Father McDonnell writes, "Christ has shared with us His Spirit, who, existing as One and the same Being in the head and in the members, vivifies, unifies and moves the whole Body" (*Toward a New Pentecost For a New Evangelization,* p. 6).

"The person who has received the sacrament of Baptism and the one who is baptized into the Holy Spirit are both good and pleasing to God. But the person who receives the baptism into the Holy Spirit moves from the 'rose bud' stage of the indwelling of the Holy Spirit obtained through water baptism into the 'rose bloom' stage of the infilling of the Holy Spirit, through Spirit baptism. They experience a new Spirit power, along with an unfolding, an awakening and a release of the 'power tools', the gifts of the Holy Spirit. What one 'sees and hears' are signs to believers and unbelievers of that outpoured power of the Spirit. They are empowered to accomplish things for God that is beyond our human capabilities" (Tape: *The Touch of the Spirit*). This is expressed in the prayer of St. Paul, who pleaded that we might be "strengthened in our inner being with power through the Spirit" (see Eph. 3:16, 17).

Receiving the Gift of the Holy Spirit

Before Pentecost, the disciples "already had some of the Spirit power and the gifts of the Holy Spirit; but because they had not yet received the Holy Spirit of Pentecost, these gifts were not fully operative. So, before Pentecost, they had many failures" (Tape: *The Touch of the Spirit*). In Mark's gospel, for example, we read that a boy was brought to the Apostles to be delivered from an evil spirit. The spirit "made the boy unable to speak...threw him to the ground...made the boy foam at the mouth...and become rigid." The father of the boy said to Jesus, "I asked your disciples to cast it out, but they could not do it" (Mark 9:18). And before Pentecost, the disciples, although followers of Jesus, had shown a weakness; they had locked themselves in the Upper Room for fear of persecution and death. But, in the words of the prophet Isaiah, "He (the Spirit) gives power to the faint and strengthens the powerless" (Is. 40:29). It was only after Pentecost that a higher level of the Spirit's power is found in the boldness and zeal of Peter and the disciples; and how effective they were in declaring God's word, praying for healings and driving out evil spirits. They received 3,000 converts that day and about 5,000 later on. Scripture says that even the shadow of Peter and clothes touched to his garments healed people (Acts 5:15).

In his letter to the Romans, St. Paul explained how the Holy Spirit witnessed and confirmed Paul's effectiveness in proclaiming the gospel in the early Church. He writes, "By the power of signs and wonders, by the power of the Spirit of God...I have fully proclaimed the good news of Christ" (Rom.15:19). And to the Thessalonians Paul writes, "Our gospel came to you, not only in word, but also in power and in the Holy Spirit and with full conviction" (1 Thess. 1:5). For those who want it, this same Spirit power is available that was given to Paul and the Apostles.

Jesus tells us in John's gospel that "the one who believes in me will do the works that I do...and even greater works than I do." (John 14:12). He was saying that, "according to your faith" (Matt. 8.13) and "without doubt" (Matt. 21:21), with that same Spirit power, you also will do signs and wonders in my name and be effective witnesses in spreading the gospel. But Jesus said that the "the love of many will grow cold" (Matt. 24:12); and he adds,

"When the Son of Man comes will he find faith on the earth?" (Luke 18:8). St. Paul encourages us in our faith, saying, "I come to you…not with plausible words of wisdom, but with demonstrations of the Spirit power, so that you faith might rest, not on human wisdom, but on the power of God" (1 Cor. 2:4).

As we allow the Holy Spirit to teach and guide us, the person of Jesus becomes real and present to us. As Jesus said, "Those who love me will be loved by my Father, and I will love them and reveal myself to them" (John 14:21).

The letter to the Hebrews reminds us that "Jesus Christ is the same yesterday, today and forever" (Heb.13:8). When Jesus says, "I will reveal myself to them" He "is not revealing anything new about Himself or any new doctrine"; (Tape: *The Touch of the Spirit*). But with the "eyes" of our heart, He is giving us a deeper spiritual revelation of which this Jesus is who has always been present in Him; a sharing in the knowledge that God has of Himself (see John 1:21). Jesus "loves us so much that He wishes to bring us into the secrecy of His own intimate life in the Trinity" (*Divine Intimacy*, p. 658).

In John's gospel, one of the disciples asked Jesus, "Lord, how is it that you will reveal yourself to us and not to the world?" Jesus answered, "Those who love me will keep my word, and my Father will love them, and we will come to them and make our abode with them" (John 14:23). "The Spirit that my Father will send is the Spirit of Truth whom the world cannot receive because it neither sees Him nor knows Him, but you know Him because He abides with you now (through water Baptism) and will be in you" later (at Pentecost) (14:17). And "I will not now call you servants, but I have called you friends because I have made known to you all that I have heard from the Father" (15:15). The disciples already had the Holy Spirit, but Jesus had promised that they would have much more on Pentecost.

The worldly-minded person cannot receive the Holy Spirit because, as Paul wrote in Romans 8:5: "Those who live according to the sinful nature have their minds set on what that nature desires." That is, they live without God as the center of their lives. They are not spiritually sensitive enough to recognize the inspira-

Receiving the Gift of the Holy Spirit

tions of the Spirit because their attention and energies are focused mainly on intellectual, social and/or material achievements. "But," Paul counters, "those who live in accordance with the Spirit have their minds set on what the Spirit desires" (*ibid*.). Jesus becomes the center and Lord of their life.

God calls each one of us to receive that same witnessing power of his Spirit of love; to have that personal and intimate experience of His "divine hug"; the intimate embrace of the love of the Father, the Son and the Holy Spirit. It is a call to a personal Pentecost; a call for repentance, spiritual renewal and a total commitment to Jesus Christ as our personal Lord and Savior; a call to be spirit-filled Christians and "effective witnesses" in the service of God's people.

In the words of the prophet Joel, "God said … 'I will pour out my spirit on all mankind… .'" Peter proclaimed, "The promise of the Spirit is for you, for your children, and for all who are far away; for everyone whom the Lord our God calls to Him" (Acts 2:39). Through the prophet Isaiah, God promised, "For I will pour out water (Holy Spirit) on the thirsty land, and streams on dry ground; I will pour my Spirit on your descendants and my blessing on your offspring" (Isaiah 44:3).

That is, God wants to pour out his Spirit on all ages, races, denominations and creeds for all time. As we receive the Baptism in the Holy Spirit, let us "throw open the windows" of our hearts and receive that personal Pentecost and experience of what Pope Paul VI called "the experience of the divine hug"—that intimate embrace of the Father, the Son and the Holy Spirit. In the words of Pope John XXIII and Pope John Paul II, "Let us be open to what the Spirit is saying to the Churches." The Vatican II document, *Lumen Gentium*, in article 12, asks those who preside over the Churches "not to extinguish the Spirit, but test all things and hold fast to what is good" (*Toward a New Pentecost For a New Evangelization*, p. 64; cf. 1 Thess. 5:12). In the book of Isaiah, God promised, "I will pour out water (the Holy Spirit) on the thirsty land." Let us ask ourselves, how thirsty are we to really want to listen to and be filled with the Holy Spirit? In the words of St. Paul, "Do not grieve the Spirit of God… do not quench the Spirit" (1 Thess. 5:19).

"We quench the Spirit when we ignore the inspirations of the Holy Spirit and the nudging of our conscious...we are preventing the flow and the infilling of the Spirit." To the Galatians Paul says, "Live by the Spirit" (Gal.5:16). And to the Ephesians, "Be filled with the Spirit" (Eph. 5:18); that is, keep on being filled with the Spirit; "fan into flame the gift of God [the Holy Spirit] that is within you through the laying on of my hands" (Eph. 4:30; 2 Timothy 1:6) (Tape: *The Touch of the Spirit*).

Receiving the Gift of the Holy Spirit

CHAPTER 8

Baptism in the Spirit—Normative for Christians

The history of the Church tells us that in the first eight centuries of the Church, Christians in general considered it normal spirituality to be baptized in the Holy Spirit and thus become charismatic. It was a normal part of their conversion experience; "persons not only asked for and received the Spirit during Christian initiation, but they expected that the Spirit would demonstrate its power by the transformation it would effect in their lives" (*Toward a New Pentecost for a New Evangelization*, p. 21). That is why, in the Acts of the Apostles, Paul asked the Ephesians, "Have you received the Holy Spirit when you were believers?" (Acts 19:2). In other words, were you baptized into the Holy Spirit? They replied, "'No, we have not so much as heard whether there is a Holy Spirit!' So, when Paul laid hands on them, the Holy Spirit came upon them, and they spoke with tongues and prophesied" (Acts 19:6). "The Ephesians' baptism into the Holy Spirit was subsequent to and distinct from their belief in Christ…and distinct, that is, separate, from water baptism" (*What Makes a Person Charismatic?*, p. 8).

The book of Acts also tells us that Peter and John were sent to Samaria because "they heard that the people had received the word of God…but that the Holy Spirit had not yet come upon them; they had only been baptized with water in the name of the Lord Jesus." So Peter and John laid hands on them and the Samaritans received the Holy Spirit (see Acts 8:15-17).

In November, 1980, Pope John Paul II received a group representing the Charismatic Renewal. Referring to some of the Pope's comments, we read in the book, *Open the Windows*, edited by Kilian Mc Donnell, O.S.B., that "The Christ-centered character of this experience of the Holy Spirit brought early Christians to the conviction that…the Holy Spirit is not to be grieved, the movement of the Spirit is not to be quenched, and Christians are to be led by the Spirit" (p. 28). The testimony of the early Church Fathers "demonstrated that the baptism into the Holy Spirit is not a matter of private piety, but of the official liturgy of the Church's public life. Historically, the baptism in the Holy Spirit is an integral part of those initiatory sacraments which are constitutive of the Church, namely, Baptism, Confirmation and the Eucharist. In this sense, the baptism into the Holy Spirit is normative." (*Toward a New Pentecost for a New Evangelization*, p. 15).

CHAPTER 9

Symbols of the Holy Spirit in Scripture

To express the various facets of the Holy Spirit's power and activities, Holy Scripture refers to the Holy Spirit as Living Water, Wind, Breath, Air, Fire, a Cloud, Light, a Seal, a Dove, and the Hand or Finger of God.

A. Living Water

1) In the gospel of John we read, "Out of the believer's heart, will flow rivers of Living Water" (John 7:38). Out of His spirit, His inner self, shall flow manifestations in the believer's life of the presence and power of the Holy Spirit in them.

2) Water is a symbol of cleansing, refreshing, and renewal. Paul wrote to Titus, "But when the goodness…of God our Savior appeared, He saved us, not because of any works of righteousness we have done, but according to His mercy, through the water of rebirth and renewal by the Holy Spirit" (Titus 3:5).

3) Through water baptism, for example, we are cleansed (washed) of original sin and, as Saint Paul wrote, we become "the temple of the Holy Spirit," (1 Cor. 3:16), the dwelling place of the Trinity, with the Holy Spirit exercising His proper role of sanctification in us.

4) As we allow the Holy Spirit to control our lives, to cleanse and renew our spirit, "put on the mind of Christ" (Phil. 2:5), and become renewed: "If anyone is in Christ, there is a new creation, everything old has passed away; see, everything has become new" (2 Cor. 5:17). We begin to think, speak, and act more like Jesus. In the fourth century, Cyril of Jerusalem, one of the early Church Fathers said, "The Spirit is a new kind of

water; what the Spirit touches, the Spirit changes. The Spirit sanctifies the Christian, transforming the baptized person into the likeness of Christ" (*Fanning the Flame*, p. 18).

5) I think that it is significant that the words "living water" and "flowing rivers" are used as symbols of the Holy Spirit and the work of purification and sanctification that He wants to accomplish in our lives. Contrary to lakes and ponds, rivers are moving bodies of water that help to clean and purify river beds and banks by carrying various kinds of debris with it; whereas lakes and ponds tend to become stagnant and not as clear. Also, rivers usually find a way to flow between, around and/or over anything that is in its way.

6) As we allow the Holy Spirit to guide, to cleanse and renew our spirit, we experience the prayer of the Psalmist, "Create in me a clean heart, O God and put right spirit within me" (Ps. 51:10). "The Holy Spirit wants to purify and cleanse us of all sin and imperfections so we can experience a life of union with the Blessed Trinity, the union (of Divine Love) that exist between the Three Divine Persons" (*Divine Intimacy*, p. 667). "This Holy Spirit of Love is given to our soul through the infinite merits of Jesus so that we may complete the work of our sanctification, and having transformed us by His charity, He leads us back to God" (p. 565).

B. Wind - Symbol of Power

1) Jesus said, "When the Holy Spirit comes on you, you shall receive power," (Acts 1:8).

2) The word spirit in Hebrew is the word "*ruah*," which means breath, wind, or sigh—each expressive of power—the power of life, the power of wind, and the power of love expressed by a sigh. On Pentecost, the book of Acts tells us of its second expression: "suddenly from heaven there came a sound like the rush of a violent wind, and it filled the entire house where they were sitting" (Acts 4:31).

3) "When the disciples had prayed, the place in which they were gathered...was shaken...and they were filled with the Holy

Spirit and spoke the word of God with boldness" (Acts 4:31)

C. Breath

1) Scripture says that God's Spirit breathed life into the clay that became Adam (Gen. 2:7).

2) When Jesus appeared to the disciples on Easter, he breathed on them and said, "Receive the Holy Spirit," the Holy Breath, a symbol of life to the church (see John 20:22).

D. Anointing With Oil

This signifies the action of the Holy Spirit in strength for sustaining its mission, in healing and in the sacraments.

1) As Part of the rite of priestly ordination of Aaron, the book of Leviticus says that "Moses took the anointing oil and anointed the tabernacle and all that was in it...and he poured some of the anointing oil on Aaron's head and anointed him, to consecrate him" (Lev. 8:10-12). Blessed oil is still used today for the anointing in administering priestly and deaconate Holy Orders, in administering the sacraments of Baptism, Confirmation and in the Sacrament of the Sick.

2) The gospel of Luke says of the baptism of Jesus in the Jordan, "God anointed Jesus of Nazareth with the Holy Spirit and with power" (Acts 10:38) (*Toward a New Pentecost for a New Evangelization*, p. 7).

3) Oil is also used for the anointing of Kings and Rulers as they ascend the throne. "Then Samuel took the horn of oil and anointed him [King David] in the presence of his brothers; and the Spirit of the Lord came mightily upon David" (1Sam. 16:13).

E. Fire

1) Fire signifies the transforming energy of Holy Spirit action in our lives.

2) John the Baptist said, "He [Jesus] will baptize you with water and with fire" (Luke 1:17).

3) On Pentecost, the Holy Spirit came as "tongues of fire" (Acts 2:3).

4) Jesus said, "I have come to cast fire on the earth; would that it he enkindled" Luke 12:49).

F. Cloud/Light

These two images sometimes appear together, at times obscure, at times luminous, revealing the presence of God while veiling his glory. For example:

1) God led his people, Israel, through the desert by a cloud by day and fire by night. (Ex. 13:21).

2) Scripture says that the Holy Spirit overshadowed Mary (reminiscent of an enveloping cloud of a divine presence), when she conceived Jesus (Luke 1:35).

3) A cloud took Jesus when he ascended to heaven (Acts 1:9).

G. Seal

This is a symbol similar to anointing with oil.

1) "The Father has set his seal on Christ" (John 6:27).

2) "It is God who establishes us with you in Christ…by putting his seal on us and giving us his spirit in our hearts as a first installment" (2 Cor. 1:22).

3) "In him also, when you have heard the word of truth, the gospel of your salvation, and had believed in him, were marked with the seal of the promised Holy Spirit" (Eph. 1:13).

4) Paul wrote to the Ephesians, "Do not grieve the Holy Spirit of God, with whom you were sealed for the day of redemption" (Eph. 4:30).

H. Hands

1) Joshua, son of Nun, was full of the Spirit of wisdom because Moses laid his hands on him (see Deut. 34:9).

2) Referring to the Samaritans who received only the word of God…and not the Holy Spirit, Peter and John laid hands on

them and they received the Holy Spirit (Acts 19:6).

3) "All those who were sick with various kinds of diseases were brought to him [Jesus]; he laid his hands on each of them and cured them" (Luke 4:40).

4) Tertullian (c. 160-225) describes the function of laying on of hands during Christian initiation, as "inviting and welcoming the Spirit" (*Toward a New Pentecost for a New Evangelization*, p. 15).

I. The Finger of God

1) "God's law written on tablets of stone by the finger of God" (Deut. 9:10).

2) "The letter from Christ...is written with the Spirit of the Living God...not on tablets of stone, but on tablets of human hearts" (2 Cor. 3:3).

3) "It is by the finger of God that Jesus cast out demons" (Luke 11:20).

J. Dove

This is the symbol of the Holy Spirit of gentle love that exists between the Father and the Son.

1) "When Jesus came up from the water of his baptism (in the Jordan River), the Holy Spirit, in the form of a dove, came down on him and remained with him" (Luke 3:22).

2) "I saw the Spirit descending from heaven like a dove and it remained on him" (John 1:32).

3) "He on whom you see the Spirit descend and remain, this is he who baptizes with the Holy Spirit" (John 1:33).

Receiving the Gift of the Holy Spirit

CHAPTER 10

Early Church Fathers on Christian Initiation and the Baptism In The Holy Spirit

Tertullian (c. 160-225)
In a treatise called On Baptism, Tertullian explained how the church in North Africa had long celebrated the rights of initiation (water bath, anointings, imposition of hands, Eucharistic celebration). He describes the function of the imposition of hands as "inviting and welcoming the Holy Spirit." Tertullian then addresses the newly baptized who are about to enter the area where all are about to celebrate the Eucharist:

"Therefore you blessed ones for whom the grace of God is waiting, when you come up from the sacred bath of the new birth, when you spread out your hands for the first time in your mother's house (Church) with your brethren, ask your Father, ask your Lord, for the special gift of his inheritance, the distribution of charisms which form an additional feature (of baptism). 'Ask,' he says 'and you shall receive.' In fact, you have sought and it has been added to you" (*Toward a New Pentecost for a New Evangelization,* p.15; *Fanning the Flame,* p.16).

Ireneus (c. 130-200)
In his writings of Against Heresies, 5:61, Ireneus supported the fact that, having received the baptism in the Holy Spirit, the early Christians experienced the various gifts of the Holy Spirit in the second century. He writes:

"We hear of many members of the Church who have prophetic gifts, and, by the Spirit, speak with all kinds of tongues, and bring men's secret thoughts to light for their own good (the "word of knowledge"), expounding the mysteries of God" (Rev. Terry Donahue, C.C., *The Gift of Tongues in the Liturgy*, p. 2).

Origen (c.185-c.254)

Origen recognizes a formal relationship between baptism and the reception of the charisms: "The water of baptism is the symbol of the purification of the soul washed of every stain of sin, and it (baptism) is by itself the principle and source of the Divine charisms for everyone who offers one's self to the Divinity through the powerful (invoking of the adorable Trinity)" (*Fanning the Flame*, p.16).

Hilary of Poitiers (c. 315-367)

Hilary describes the experience of the gifts of the Holy Spirit. He seems to indicate that receiving the baptism in the Holy Spirit was still a common practice and part of the spirituality of the early Church. He writes: we who have been reborn through the sacrament of baptism experience intense joy when we feel within us the first stirrings of the Holy Spirit. Concerning the use of the gifts, Hilary writes, "We begin to have insights into the mysteries of faith, we are able to prophesy and to speak with wisdom... and receive the gift of healing" (*Fanning the Flame*, p. 17).

Cyril of Jerusalem (c. 315-387)

Cyril thought "that the Church of Jerusalem, as all others, stands in a charismatic succession in a history of the Spirit beginning with Moses." He writes, "The Spirit is a new kind of water; what the Spirit touches, the Spirit changes...He appeals to the experience of the church in Jerusalem...and to the whole world." Cyril says, "They were without anything wanting...baptized in all fullness" (*Fanning the Flame*, p. 18).

John Chrysostom (c. 347-407)

Chrysostom represented the Syrian Liturgy in Antioch. According to him, the model of the Apostolic Church had the reception of charisms (Gifts of the Holy Spirit) within the Liturgy: "Whoever was baptized spoke in tongues... many prophesied... among other charisms received at initiation in the apostolic age were wisdom and healing." Chrysostom complained, however, that "the charisms are long gone." In the 4th Century, we begin to see the decline of the uses of the gifts of the Holy Spirit. Witnessing this, he writes: "The present is like a woman who has fallen from her former prosperous days. In many respects, she retains only the tokens of the ancient prosperity" (*Fanning the Flame*, p. 19; *Toward a New Pentecost for a New Evangelization,* p. 17).

Joseph Hazzaya (c. 710-713)

Hazzaya, one of the great Syrian mystics, writes of the "signs through which you feel that the Spirit received in baptism is working in you," mentioning "a flow of spiritual speech (tongues)" and a knowledge of both worlds (word of knowledge or wisdom) in addition to jubilation... or praise (*Fanning the Flame*, p. 20).

Receiving the Gift of the Holy Spirit

CHAPTER 11

Reasons for the Decline in the Use of the Charisms

The enthusiasm and power experienced by the Church in apostolic times began to diminish over the centuries for various reasons, such as the abuses that Paul had seen and anticipated (see 1 Cor. 12:1; 14:20), and the arrival of age of monasticism that emphasized the personal (non-charismatic) gifts of the Spirit in a way that unfortunately displaced rather than shored up the use of the charismatic gifts. Some "charismatic heresies," like Montanism, arose to staunch the flow of the Spirit. Its fullest restoration will be seen in the future, as proclaimed by Joel (2:28-29). Even some saints misinterpreted the plan of God in the timing of the manifestation of the gifts:

1. Suggesting that even these "tokens" of charisms are no longer needed, St. John Chrysostom writes:

    "In the beginning, charisms were given even to the unworthy, because the ancient period needed this help to foster the faith, but now, they are not even given to the worthy because the faith is strong and firm enough not to need the support" (*In Principium Actorum*, quoted by Rev. Terry Donahue, C.C. in *The Gift of Tongues in the Liturgy*).

2. About the end of the 2nd century, there was a heresy called Montanism. This heresy exaggerated the importance of prophesy and other gifts of the Holy Spirit. Because the Church was concerned about the use of the gifts being associated with the heresy of Montanism, the using the gifts was not encouraged (Rev. Terry Donahue, C.C., *The Gift of Tongues in the Liturgy*).

3. Another reason was the practice of infant baptism. Infants received the grace of baptism, but could not experience the full

manifestation of the grace and personal experience of Pentecost until adulthood (Rev. Terry Donahue, C.C., *The Gift of Tongues in the Liturgy*).

4. Also, at the end of the 2nd century, the gifts of the Holy Spirit were associated with only the clergy, not with the whole church (Rev. Terry Donahue, C.C., *The Gift of Tongues in the Liturgy*).

5. According to Martin Kelsey, in the 4th century, Augustine viewed the gift of tongues as a sign needed only for apostolic times "and it (tongues) passed away." When discussing baptism, he clearly did not expect anyone to speak in tongues: "For who expects in these days that those on whom hands are laid, that they may receive the Holy Spirit, should forthwith begin to speak with tongues?" (Rev. Terry Donahue, C.C., *The Gift of Tongues in the Liturgy*); *Tongue Speaking: An Experiment in Spiritual Experience*, Martin T. Kelsey).

6. Joseph Hazzaya, a Syrian Mystic of the 8th Century, associated the gift of tongues only with the heights of holiness, especially in monasteries... saying that "from the state of wonder, you will derive a flow of spiritual speech" (the gift of tongues) (Rev. Terry Donahue, C.C., *The Gift of Tongues in the Liturgy*).

7) One of the differences between the early Church community and the community of Christians in the church today is that the Church today does not have the same full "awareness, expectation and openness" for the need for a greater desire for more of the fullness of Christian spirituality (*Towards a New Pentecost*, p. 23). It is hoped that the Life in the Spirit Seminars will help Christians today to have that same great awareness, expectation and openness to that need of the power of the Holy Spirit in their lives today as did the early Christians; and that the Baptism into the Holy Spirit will again "fan into flame" more of the fullness and manifestations of that Spirit power already in them through water Baptism.

St. John's gospel tells us that the "Spirit is given without measure" (John 3:34). But because of our human limitations, we cannot receive the Spirit without measure. It is as if we are a little bucket trying to scoop up all of that vast infinite ocean of God's personal Love for us. And we find that we cannot submerge the little bucket and empty out that ocean of love, because God's Spirit of Love for us is much more than we can hold or understand. But Jesus wants to fill us with that His Love. He tells us "Let anyone who is thirsty…and believes in me…come to me and drink…Out of the believer's heart shall flow rivers of living water. Now he said this of the Spirit which believers in him were to receive" (John 7:37). This indicates that there will be some external manifestations of the power of the Spirit flowing out of that person as a behavioral characteristic. Even the very presence of that person will radiate that Spirit Power. Through the Baptism in the Holy Spirit Jesus invites us to "come to him" as the Baptizer into the Holy Spirit. Depending upon our faith and openness, we can have that same infilling Spirit power had by the early Christians. "The book of Acts tells us that 'the promise is for you and your children' (Acts 2:39). And like them, we not only seek and receive the Spirit, but, we too, can expect demonstrations of that Spirit power and transformation in our own lives" (*Fanning the Flame*, p. 16).

CHAPTER 12

Statements of the Popes on the Charismatic Renewal and the Baptism in The Holy Spirit

From the highest level of Church authority come the endorsement and approval of the Charismatic Renewal. The Holy Spirit moves within the Body of the Church; we are the members of the Body of the Church, of which Christ is the head. This is a sign that the Holy Spirit is working in the Church.

1961: Pope John XXIII formally called together the Vatican II Council to be held in l962 (*Open the Windows*, p. 1).

1962: The Vatican Council was held. Pope John XXIII called to mind the scene of the apostles gathered in Jerusalem…waiting for the promised Spirit…for which he added a prayer for a New Pentecost (in the Church). Part of the prayer reads: "Renew your wonders in our time, as though for a new Pentecost and together with Mary, the Mother of Jesus, and also under the guidance of Saint Peter, we pray for increase the reign of the Divine Savior…the reign of truth…justice…love and peace. Amen" (*Open the Windows*, p. 1). The Council "opened the windows" to allow the fresh breath of the Holy Spirit to renew and refresh the spiritual life of the Church.

In the words of Fathers McDonnell and Montague, "From our experience, the greatest area of concern is the need for a more fully evangelized and evangelizing community. …the disintegration of family life, the decrease in priestly and religious vocations, wasteful consumption, forgetfulness of the poor—these and many other factors are symptoms of the Catholic community's weakened state.

It has left the community prey to the pressures of a secular world where media repeatedly mock the gospel and cheapen the centrality of a person's worth as a child of God. The need for conversion is evident" (*Fanning the Flame*, p. 10).

1) A weakened community will not easily provide the environment necessary for families to communicate the faith to the next generation, nor to foster the vocations needed to serve the Church.

2) It will not reclaim the great losses experienced within various ethnic groups attracted by other church groups.

3) Will not bring a vibrant faith to our revised liturgical rites, nor support the type of parish that fosters life in the Spirit.

4) Such a community cannot evangelize effectively, cannot hand on its faith to its own children, and cannot reach out to those who have drifted away, so to fulfill the church's mission and identity (*Fanning the Flame*, p. 11).

5) "An indispensable element in a renewed parish is ongoing conversion in the lives of the pastor and parish staff. Pastoral leaders must have not only the vision for the spiritually-renewed parish, but the personal experience that will enable them to witness and minister the life of the baptism in the Spirit to others" (*Fanning the Flame*, p. 24). It is hoped that the Life in the Spirit Seminars can be an instrument for spiritual renewal and for the answering of the prayer of John XXIII who asked us to pray for the Council. "Renew in our day, O Lord, your wonders as in a new Pentecost" (*Open the Windows*, p. 1).

Pope succeeding Pope John XXIII continued his vision for spiritual renewal in the Church. A total of 16 documents, promulgated between 1962 and 1992, referring to the Holy Spirit and the spiritual renewal for the Church, were accepted and signed by three of the popes that reigned during that period: Pope John XXIII, Pope Paul VI, and Pope John Paul II. "This small collection of documents do not necessarily refer only to the Charismatic Renewal, but the Renewal has understood itself as one of the effects of Pope John XXIII throwing open the windows to let the strong breath of

God renew the Church. This attitude seems to have been accepted by Pope VI and John Paul II" (*Open the Windows,* p. 5).

1964: The Second Vatican Council—*The Decree on the Apostolate of the Laity*, (Pope John XXIII): "The Holy Spirit sanctifies the people of God through the ministry of the sacraments. However, for the exercise of the apostolate, the Holy Spirit gives the faithful special gifts besides the sacraments. From the reception of these gifts of the Spirit, even the most ordinary ones, there arises for each of the faithful, the right and the duty of exercising those gifts in the church and in the world for the good of humans and the development of the church. The laity have the obligation to nourish themselves and hopefully to be guided in that by charism of teaching given primarily, but not exclusively, to the clergy. Paul tells the Corinthians, that 'the Spirit gives (these gifts) to each one as he wills...for the building up of the whole body in charity'" (1 Cor. 12:11).

1973: Pope Paul VI: "The invigorating breath of the Spirit has come to awaken the slumbering energies in the Church; to reawaken, to arouse sleeping charisms (gifts of the Spirit); to instill that sense of vitality and joy, which at every period of history, defines the Church, herself as young and of topical interest, ready and happy to proclaim again her eternal message to the new times (of the new evangelization)." He called the Charismatic Renewal "an old expression of a new reality which points to a transformed humankind" (*Open the Windows*, p. 11).

1975: Pope Paul VI (at the *First International Charismatic Conference*):
"There are a very large number of baptized persons, who, for the most part, have not formally renounced their baptism, but, who are entirely indifferent to it. The resistance (of this group) takes the form of inertia and slightly hostile attitude of the person who feels that he is one of the family who claim to know it all and have tried it all and who no longer believe it" (*Open the Windows*, p.19; *Evangelization In the Modern World*, Art. 6).

Receiving the Gift of the Holy Spirit

1975: Pope Paul VI, speaking in four languages to 10,000 Catholic charismatics, with two cardinals and 10 bishops present, stated that no Catholic can expect to receive the baptism in the Holy Spirit by simply going to Mass on Sunday, nor by merely being educated in the Catholic school system. He said that no Catholic can receive the baptism in the Holy Spirit by simply receiving the sacraments. So receiving the baptism in the Holy Spirit involved a totally different spiritual experience—one of a new and deeper personal relationship with Jesus by the Power of the Holy Spirit. (*First Charismatic Conference in Rome*) (Tape: *The Touch of the Spirit*).

1975: Pope Paul VI extended a "mandate" for Catholics to evangelize and spread the Charismatic Movement throughout the world, "so that the Holy Spirit can do the work He wants to do in the church." He called the Charismatic Renewal "a chance for the Church and the world," (*Open the Windows,* p. 10; *First International Charismatic Congress*, Rome, 1975). This is a strong statement indicating that the Church should be aware of this favored moment and not let it go unexploited (*Touch of the Spirit*, p.10).

1975: Pope Paul VI: "I desire that the leaders see the renewal, not as a movement, but as the church itself." The need for a perpetual Pentecost is great. Baptism in the Holy Spirit is the very heart of the Charismatic Renewal and a renewal of a Perpetual Pentecost. It introduces the believer into the flow of love by which the Father loves the Son in the Holy Spirit" (Open the Windows, p. 9; *International Leaders Conference*).

1981: Pope John Paul II: Pope John Paul II said that many Christians have not progressed beyond that first stage of empowerment by the Holy Spirit that was characterized by water baptism. "They have never made a personal commitment in faith to Jesus as their personal Lord and Savior" (*4th Inter. Leader's Conference*). He also referred to several principles emphasized by Pope Paul VI in l975, namely:

1) Be guided by holy discernment; "Test everything and hold fast

Statements of the Popes on the Charismatic Renewal and the Baptism in The Holy Spirit

of what is good" (1 Thess. 5:21);

2) Maintain fidelity to the Faith under the magisterium of the Church;

3) Value the higher gifts—which are given in service for the higher good.

4) Pursue charity, which alone brings about Christian perfection.

1983: Pope John Paul II describes the role of priests in the renewal as "unique and indispensable." He encourages them to be open to the renewal, to be open to sacramental ministry, to maintain the renewal within the mainstream of the Church. Priests cannot minister to the Renewal unless they adopt a welcoming attitude to it. To the Bishops he said, "Your role is to encourage the renewal" (*Open the Windows*, Doc. 12; pp.10 and 15).

Cardinal Bernadine, when archbishop of Chicago, said, "Priests have a pastoral obligation to encourage the laity to seek an ever increasing intensity of the Charismatic gifts of the Spirit; to seek earnestly the continued advance, the enhancement of the gifts of the Spirit." In the words of St. Paul, "...to each is given the manifestation of the Spirit for the common good...who allots these gifts...as the Spirits chooses" (1Cor. 12:7, 11).

1980: "Pope John Paul II referred to the Baptism in the Spirit as the 'effusion of the Spirit' and acknowledged that those in the Renewal owe to it a 'deeper and deeper experience of Christ.' This clearly shows that the Baptism in the Holy Spirit is a Christ-centered event" (*Open the Windows*, p. 28).

The Pope commends participants in the Renewal to the protection of Mary who conceived Jesus through the power of the Holy Spirit. To re-discover Pentecost is to find Mary. This is not just a theological insight, but reflects the experience of the renewal at the international level (*Open the Windows*, p. 29).

The first Pentecost did not occur outside the church, but in the midst of the church gathered with Mary in expectant prayer. The theme of Mary and Pentecost will be one which will occupy the renewal. Pope John Paul II mentioned in every address to a charismatic group a remark about Mary, (*Open the Windows*, p. 10).

1980: John Paul II: "Invoking upon you and your commitment the loving and assiduous protection of her (Mary) who, through the Holy Spirit, conceived in her womb and gave birth to the incarnate Son of God (Luke 1:35), I willingly grant you my Apostolic Blessing to extend it to all those who are members of the movement, and to all the persons who are dear to you in the Lord" (*Open the Windows*, p. 28; *Audience with Italian Charismatics*).

1982: John Paul II stated that the Renewal is a sign that prayer has returned to its place in the life of the Church. Through Mary, the Mother of the Church, the Holy Spirit is leading persons to find again joy and the power of their new baptism" (*Open the Windows*, p. 28).

1984: John Paul II said, "In celebrating Pentecost we find Mary in the midst of the Apostles. She is the one who accepted the Spirit's greatest Gift, the life of Jesus. Mary, who is the Mother of the Church, should be the mother and the model of the Renewal in the Church" (*Open the Windows*, p. 48).

1987: "Pope John Paul II reminded the *6th International Leaders Conference* that 'the history of the Church is at the same time the history of two thousand years of the action of the Holy Spirit,' (Doc. 19). The Spirit is always doing a new thing" (*Open the Windows*, p. 10).

1984: Pope John Paul II reminded the conference of Leaders that they are called to share in the Church's vocation to evangelize in their local churches (*5th International Leaders' Conference*).

1992: Pope John Paul II stated, "Since the gifts of the Holy Spirit are given for the building up of the church, you, as leaders of the Charismatic Renewal are challenged to seek increasingly effective ways in which the various groups you represent and manifest their complete communion of mind and heart with the Apostolic See and the College of Bishops, and cooperate more fruitfully in the Church's mission in the world" (in a talk to the leaders of the Council of the International Catholic Charismatic Renewal Office, Rome).

A statement of the Bishop's Liaison Committee with the Catholic Charismatic Renewal, said, "To a great extent the success of the Renewal depends on an informed, balanced, mature, doctrinally sound leadership, especially at the local and diocesan levels" (*Pastoral Statement on the Catholic Charismatic Renewal*).

1992: Pope John Paul II referred to the coalescence of the charismatic Church with the institutional Church: "Since it is the Spirit himself who guides those he has established as Bishops to care for the Church of God, (Acts 20:28), there can be no conflict between fidelity to the Church and her magisterium. Speaking of the authority in the Church and the successors of the Apostles, Peter, we can apply the words of Jesus, 'You are Peter, and upon this rock I will build my Church and the gates of hell shall not prevail against it' (Matt.16-18); and 'he who listens to you, listens to me; he who rejects you rejects me and rejects the one who sent me'" (Luke 10:16).

Receiving the Gift of the Holy Spirit

CHAPTER 13

Why You Should Pray in Tongues

I like the whimsical story about the dog that entered an office with a job application in his mouth. The surprised and skeptical office manager tested the dog for the required typing skills and computer savvy, tests that the dog passed with amazing proficiency. The astounded manager asked the dog, as a final requirement, if he were bilingual—to which the dog responded, "Meow!"

Knowing a second language can be, in certain situations, a tremendous asset. And that is true in a most special way when addressing God in prayer. Of course God understands any and every language. Yet he invites us to use a special "extra language" of his choice, not ours, which is not just God-chosen but also God-articulated; it is a language that expresses our praise of him in a way that far transcends our limited natural ability to do so. Paul describes this awesome language, in which God prays to God with our human speech:

"The Spirit helps us in our weakness. We do not know what we are to pray for, but the Spirit himself intercedes for us with groans that words cannot express. And he who searches our hearts knows the mind of the Spirit, because the Spirit intercedes for the believers in accordance with God's will" (Rom. 8:26-27).

Paul goes even further in describing, in 1 Cor. 14, this prayer language, and advocating its use not just for some but for everyone (verse 5). As the Lord "searches our hearts," this gift language is custom-designed for each person, with sometimes more than one language for the same individual. It thus expresses God's very personal love and concern for each of us, as a parent shows a different kind of concern for each child in the family. Having reminded the Romans that praying in tongues (a phenomenon called glossolalia) assures us that in our petitions we are seeking God's will and not necessarily our own, he then urges the Ephesians to frame their petitions in their heavenly language: "Pray in the Spirit on all occasions with all kinds of prayers and requests" (Eph. 6:18). Jude reminds us in his epistle (v. 20), that the mountain-moving faith that should animate those petitions is itself fostered by the use of tongues.

These sacred writers knew that Jesus had promised that all "believers" would be able to speak in new tongues (Mark 16:17), but they still felt compelled to remind and encourage believers to do so. Even Pope John Paul II has encouraged it as part of the baptism in the Spirit experience—which he himself received at the age of eleven, as he related in a talk to charismatic leaders in Rome. Christians today are less faith-motivated than the early Christians who treasured this charism (see Acts 2:4; 10:46; 19:6), and even used it liturgically in their celebration of the Mass. While every believer is "able" to pray in tongues, as Jesus said, still most Christians today, tragically, are unwilling to pray in tongues; they won't even attempt to do so. In the plaintive words of the Lord, they are "a people without understanding" (Hos.4:14).

In view of all this, whenever the question is asked as to why this precious gift of God is so neglected today, the answer is: The tragic neglect of God's gift is usually not malice, but simple ignorance and prejudice—the most pernicious suppressors of truth. These two negative factors are extremely difficult to overcome, as Pope Paul VI reminded us when encouraging the restoration of the charisms that were prominent in the early Church. Today's Christians are "a people without understanding" about all 25 of the charismatic gifts listed in the New Testament, of which the gift of tongues is the gateway—the "entrée gift" that facilitates the reception of all the other charismatic gifts, such as healing.

In an attempt to confront this widespread ignorance and unwitting prejudice, let me here present a brief overview of the gift of tongues, based on God's holy word. The gift itself is designed to convince unbelievers (1 Cor. 14:22), which it actually did at Pentecost, where it converted 3000 unbelievers to become Christians (Acts 2:41). Yet, realistically, I still don't expect to convince every reader, even with Scripture quotes to supplement those already referred to; after all, Jesus himself found that he couldn't convince all of his hearers: "I told you, but you still do not believe" (John 10:25).

Four Forms of the Gift of Tongues

Paul describes, in Chapter 14 of First Corinthians, four forms of this gift, which I'll briefly outline here with corresponding scriptural references:

First: Praying in tongues (praying individually or as a group— v.2);

Second: Singing in tongues (prayer sung individually or by group— v. 15);

Third: Speaking (publicly) in tongues—a message from God to the assembly through one person's public utterance in a foreign language, to be made intelligible (equivalently translated) by a supplementary gift called interpretation of tongues; the interpretation may be presented by that same tongue-speaker (v. 13) or someone else (vs. 27-28).

Fourth: Tongues as a "proof for unbelievers"—one type of public message in a foreign language, to be "interpreted" into the vernacular, by which the Spirit "convicts" into conversion any nonbelievers who may be present (vs. 22-23).

Of these four forms of tongues, the first two (man-to-God utterances) are prayer activities that can be turned on or off like a faucet, and are available to anyone baptized in the Spirit for their personal spiritual development (v.4). The other two forms (God-to-man utterances) involve speaking in tongues, not praying in tongues, and are thus assigned to certain persons chosen by God's sovereign providence, as Paul notes in 1 Cor. 12:30, for the welfare of the community (14:5 and 26). These forms can be used authentically only when under an anointing of the Spirit for that function (v. 13and 37). He adds that speaking in tongues (not praying in tongues) is useless without an accompanying interpretation (see 14:9 and 19), which makes it equivalent to an inspired prophecy (v.5); hence, if no interpretation is forthcoming, one is to revert to praying in tongues (14:28).

Growth in the Use of the Gift of Tongues

This gift has not only these various forms or expressions, but also various levels of maturity or development. Usually a beginner prays on the first level, often referred to as "para-linguistic"; sounds have not yet developed into an articulate cadenced language, but are only repetitive babble-like utterances. Yet if one is mentally praising God by "praying with one's spirit" (1 Cor. 14:15), then this "babbling" couches prayer as the initial "vessel" of the gift of tongues. At this first stage, one should strive to articulate syllables clearly and non-repetitively and prayerfully, to enable this "devout babble" to grow into a more enriching and spiritually fulfilling stage of the gift called the "linguistic" stage.

At this point it becomes a real (living or dead) language, but usually still not understood by the speaker, although sometimes by others nearby who might be familiar with that language—as occurred at Pentecost (Acts 2:6). (Even when unrecognizable, the particular language at this second stage of development can be shown to be "syntactic"—as was done at the University of Michigan, where computerized measurement of the mathematical sequence of the words and phrases consistently revealed a structured linguistic "syntax.")

The third level of development is the "*Jubilus*" stage, referred to by St. Ambrose and others. (The derived word "yodel" describes a corrupted musical art form spawned from this level of tongues, as used in the Bavarian Alps.) When used in its original prayer form, this very rare but very highly Spirit-charged jubilant worship and praise in tongues usually foments within the assembly many astonishing conversions and healings of bodies, marriages, etc.

The highest level of tongues is "ecstatic utterance," used prototypically by the Hesychastic Fathers at Mount Athos and elsewhere, especially in the fourteenth century. With the sustained use of this level of praying in tongues, the person is catapulted into a deep contemplative mystical prayer experience. In this very sublime level of the gift of tongues, the Holy Spirit "dissolves" the vocal utterances into a wordless, simple, yet very profound contemplation, in a sacred silence reminiscent of Psalm 46:10: "Be

Why You Should Pray in Tongues

still and know that I am God."

I have had the privilege of personally witnessing many remarkable signs of divine approval of the precious gift of tongues, especially in its fourth form, as a "proof for unbelievers" (1 Cor. 14: 22). Let me cite a few examples.

While chaplaining one of my charismatic pilgrimages to the Holy Land, our group was praying in tongues in the tour bus, when our Israeli guide became fascinated by the utterances of one of our pilgrims (who knew only English and a little Portuguese). He understood her prayer language, and said that she was praising God in a rare dialect of Hebrew used in only two small villages in Israel—one of which we were actually passing at that moment!

A Japanese war bride, pressured to attend a charismatic prayer meeting in San Francisco by her American husband, heard an American behind her praying in Japanese, addressing her by her secret temple name, and inviting her to become a Christian and receive Jesus as her savior.

On one occasion, a skeptical Greek-rite priest affirmed that the prayer tongue of an Irish layman was the Eucharistic prayer of the Greek rite liturgy.

A nun who had doubts about the validity of the gift in a prayer meeting, was convinced when she heard a small Italian boy praying in Gaelic. In these cases (only a few of many I have witnessed), the persons praying in tongues experienced what Paul describes in 1 Cor. 14:14; they were unaware of the meaning of their utterances, but were aware that they were glorifying God.

I urge all who are reading this to ask for (or renew) the baptism in the Spirit, as Jesus urges (Luke 11:13), and at that time also to "yield" to the gift of tongues by simply babbling like a baby; becoming simple and humble like a little child, as Jesus commands (Matt. 18:3); God will bless your humility in being ready to be a "fool for Christ" (1 Cor 3:18). But keep in mind that your babbling must be prayerful, with your mind praising God (14:14); otherwise it will not become the gift of tongues but only a developed skill at babbling.

Once you receive this precious gift, use it formally, as in prayer meetings, or informally, as when driving, washing dishes, etc, like any charism, if you don't use it you can lose it. It will open up for you new dimensions of power in your prayer—in your petition prayer, deliverance prayer, worship prayer, etc. As it enriches your spiritual life more and more, you'll find that you have one more thing to thank God for—that very heavenly language itself.

CHAPTER 14

Some Benefits of Receiving the Baptism in the Holy Spirit

The benefits or fruits of receiving the Baptism in the Holy Spirit will vary with each individual, parish and community, as well as the effectiveness of its spin-off power of evangelizing.

These benefits depend not only on our awareness of the indwelling presence of the Holy Spirit already in us, through the sacrament of Baptism, but, more importantly, on our openness, faith and expectations in the additional power based on the promise of Jesus, "You shall receive power when the Holy Spirit comes on you" (Acts 1:8); that is, when receiving the gift of the Holy Spirit through Spirit baptism.

Like the early Christians, we "should not only ask for and receive more of the Holy Spirit's power, but also expect the Holy Spirit to demonstrate his power by the transformation it would effect in our lives" (*Toward A New Pentecost*, p. 21).

Some of the benefits received through the Baptism in the Holy Spirit include personal benefits, parish/community benefits, and benefits that forward evangelization. Let us consider each of these.

A. Personal Benefits

1) The Spirit-baptized person has the awesome experience of receiving the gift of the Holy Spirit Himself—being caught up, as it were, and immersed ("baptized") into the "crossfire" of the infinite personified Love that exists between the Father and the Son. This personified Love is divine: "God is Love. Whoever lives in love, lives in God and God in him" (1 John 4:16). As we remain in this awesome state we can be said to "abide" in Jesus' Spirit, with an experience of what Jesus himself described: "As the Father loves me, so also, I love you. *Abide in*

my Love" (John 15:9). This marvelous state was described by Paul: "The Love of God has been poured into our hearts through the Holy Spirit that has been given to us" (Rom. 5:5).

Through the Baptism in the Holy Spirit, Jesus immerses us, dips us, as it were, into the flow of the mutual Love that exists between the Father and the Son" (Tape: *The Touch of the Spirit*). In the words of Pope Pius VI, the essence of receiving the Baptism in the Holy Spirit is the awesome "experience of the Divine Hug."

2) Spirit Baptism deepens our awareness that the Baptism in the Holy Spirit is a Christ-centered event; this is because it is only Jesus who baptizes into the Holy Spirit (see Matt. 3:11; Mark 1:8; Luke 3:16), not a prayer leader or the group praying over the candidates.

"In 1975, Pope Pius VI referred to the Baptism in the Holy Spirit as the 'effusion of grace' and acknowledged that those in the Renewal owe to it 'a deeper and deeper experience of Christ.' This is a clear statement that the Baptism in the Holy Spirit is a Christ-centered event" (*Open the Windows*, p. 28).

3) "Spirit baptism brings the water-baptized person from encompassing the *indwelling stage* of the presence of the Holy Spirit, (received through the sacrament of Baptism), over and above the committed "born again" stage, into the *infilling stage* of the Holy Spirit, and thus into the charismatic dimension of Christian spirituality.

"This spiritual transformation brings the baptized person into a higher level of personal intimacy with the Holy Spirit, as Jesus told his disciples in John 14:17: 'the Holy Spirit lives *with* you (now)'; but he added, 'the Holy Spirit 'will be *within* you' (later)—that is, on Pentecost. To restate the often used example, the 'indwelling or infant stage' of Christian spirituality is that 'rosebud' that gradually unfolds or opens up into the 'rose bloom' of a spirit-filled Christian and into the charismatic dimension of Christian spirituality" (Tape: *The Touch of the Spirit*).

4) "Spirit baptism deepens the realization that we are a living

Some Benefits of Receiving the Baptism in the Holy Spirit

tabernacle of the indwelling Trinity; that we are constantly enveloping a God of Love who loves each one of us as though each of us were the only person in the world" (Tape: *The Touch of the Spirit*). St. Augustine said that God loves each of us as if there were only one of us.

5) The Spirit-baptized Christian is more deeply empowered to give witness to the fact that receiving the baptism in the Holy Spirit is a needed and normal and normative part of Christian spirituality.

   The testimony of the early Church Fathers "demonstrated that the Holy Spirit is not a matter of private piety, but of the official liturgy of the Church's public life. Historically, the baptism into the Holy Spirit is an integral part of those initiatory sacraments...Baptism, Confirmation and the Eucharist. In this sense, the Baptism into the Holy Spirit is normative" (*Toward a New Pentecost for a New Evangelization*, p.15). Tertullian, one of the early Church Fathers, describes the imposition of hands as "inviting and welcoming the Spirit" (*Fanning the Flame*, p. 16).

6) The Spirit baptized experiences a new grace and Spirit power to break old sinful habits and to experience a new process of spiritual transformation, as Paul told the Spirit-filled Ephesians: "You were taught to put away your former self...and to be renewed in the Spirit of your mind...to clothe yourself with the new self according to the likeness of God in true righteousness and holiness" (Eph. 4:23-24).

7) Spirit baptism helps us to become holier faster and have a more personal and intimate union with God. "The Spirit was sent on the day of Pentecost in order that he might forever sanctify the Church; thus all believers would have access to the Father through Christ in the one Spirit (Eph. 2:18).

8) "Spirit baptism helps us to become more aware of and accept our human weaknesses. We begin to more readily surrender ourselves to the guidance and transforming work of the Holy Spirit in us, believing in the words of St. Paul, that, 'he who

has begun a good work in me will bring it to completion'" (Phil. 1:6) (*Toward A New Pentecost and a New Evangelization*, p. 21).

9) The Spirit-baptized Christian is "not just joining another movement, but is embracing more of the fullness of Christian life in the Church" (*Fanning The Flame*, p. 22). As Paul reminds us, "Those who live by the Spirit set their minds on the things of the Spirit" (Rom. 8:15).

10) Spirit baptism increases the "awareness, expectation and openness" of the baptized for the "need for a (greater) desire for more of the fullness of the Spirit and Christian spirituality."

11) The baptism in the Holy Spirit gives a new and deeper father/child love relationship with God. "You have not been given a spirit of slavery...but have been given a Spirit of adoption whereby we cry, Abba, Father" (Rom 8:15). And "because you are children, God sent the Spirit of his Son into our hearts, crying Abba, Father" (Gal. 4:6).

12) Spirit-baptized persons not only know about Jesus, but experience a deeper and more personal relationship with Jesus as a real Person here and now. St. Paul writes, "...Christ loved *me*...and delivered himself for *me*" (Gal. 2:20). Jesus tells us in John's gospel that "those who love me will be loved by my Father and I will love them and reveal myself to them" (John 14:21). And, "I call you friends because I have made known to you all that I have heard from my Father" (John 15:15).

13) Assuming one has had the "born again" experience, the Spirit-baptized person experiences a new and ever-deepening conversion and commitment to Jesus Christ as his personal Lord and Savior. To receive the Spirit is to be moved to and to move others to the recognition that Jesus Christ is Lord (*Toward a New Pentecost and a New Evangelization*, p. 8). "No one can say that Jesus Christ is Lord except by the Spirit" (1Cor. 12:3).

14) The Spirit-baptized Christian experiences the promise of Jesus: "You shall receive *power* when the Holy Spirit comes on you...You shall be my witnesses...to the ends of the earth";

Some Benefits of Receiving the Baptism in the Holy Spirit

that is, that anointing power had by the early Christians to be effective witnesses to Christ and in spreading the gospel; what one sees and hears are signs to the believer and unbeliever of that power of the outpouring of the Spirit. "He (Jesus) opened their minds to understand the scriptures.... You are witnesses to these things. Stay here in the city until you are clothed with power from on high" (Luke 24:48-49).

15) Spirit baptism awakens, releases and empowers the original sacramental graces and gifts of the Holy Spirit already present in us. McDonnell and Montague explain that "the baptism in the Holy Spirit is by no means a second baptism." The Spirit-baptized person experiences "the awakening of (and release and empowerment of) the original sacramental graces (and gifts) of the Holy Spirit already present in us through the sacraments of Baptism and Confirmation" (*Fanning The Flame*, p. 9). "These gifts are activated by the same Spirit" (1 Cor. 12:7-11).

16) The Spirit baptism inspires a greater love of the Church. It has brought many back to a deeper appreciation and commitment to the inner order, sacramental life and to the teaching authority of the Church (*Toward a New Pentecost and a New Evangelization*, p. 1).

17) Spirit baptism gives us a deeper sense of obedience, love, reverence and faith in the words of Jesus to St. Peter, the first Pope, and to his successors: "Whoever listens to you, listens to me; whoever rejects you, rejects me and rejects the One who sent me" (Luke 10:16).

18) Spirit baptism helps us to mature in the fruit of the Spirit. "The fruit of the Spirit is like the segments of an orange. From the Spirit of Love, we experience the fruits of joy, peace, patience, gentleness, kindness, faithfulness, generosity, and self-control. A truly Spirit-filled person will manifest these fruits of love (spiritual behavior patterns) in a very high degree. These fruits are more important for our sanctification than are the nine classical charismatic gifts of the Holy Spirit. (Tape: *The Touch of the Spirit*).

19) As with the early Christians, Spirit baptism inspires a deeper love, hunger and appreciation for the living word of God through which the Holy Spirit nourishes and guides us (Heb.6:4-5). "They (early Christians) devoted themselves to the Apostles teaching" (Acts 2:42). "You have been born anew...by the living and abiding word of God" (1 Peter 1:23).

20) The experience of the power of the Spirit effects a radical change in the lives of many. "A new heart I will give you...and a new Spirit I will put within you...I will remove from your body a heart of stone...I will put my Spirit within you" (Ezek. 36:26-27). In the words of the early Church Father, Cyril of Jerusalem, "The Spirit is a new kind of water; what the Spirit touches, the Spirit changes...transforming the baptized into the likeness of Christ" (*Fanning the Flame*, p. 18).

21) Spirit baptism empowers us to "manifest a courageous faith, (zeal and boldness) animated by a new Love (Holy Spirit) which enables one to undertake and accomplish great thing beyond one's natural capacities for the Kingdom of God (*Toward a New Pentecost and a New Evangelization*, p.28).

22) The personal and intimate love relationship with God inspires and empowers the baptized to reach out and share that Love for the healing of the brokenness and woundedness of others.

23) Spirit baptism empowers the ministry of priest (and the Laity) and gives a new appreciation of the vocation to the priesthood and the religious life. Priests and religious have found a deeper sense of their ministry and a new meaning to their calling (*Toward a New Pentecost and a New Evangelization*, p. 63).

24) Through Spirit baptism and a personal love encounter with Jesus, "many experience a healing of personal relationships in marriage, in the family and in professional contacts (*Toward a New Pentecost*, p. 1).

25) "The baptism in the Holy Spirit fosters a new appreciation of the evidence for Mary's presence at Pentecost and her relationship (and role) in the Church" (*Toward a New Pentecost and a New Evangelization*, p. 1). "The first Pentecost did not

Some Benefits of Receiving the Baptism in the Holy Spirit

occur outside of the Church, but in the midst of the Church, gathered with Mary in expectant prayer" (Pope Paul VI, 2nd *International Leaders Conference*, 1975). Mary, who is the Mother of the Church, should be the Mother and model of the renewal in the Church. (Pope John Paul II, 5th *International Leaders Conference*, 1984).

26) The baptism in the Holy Spirit gives the baptized a new hunger and deeper dimension of prayer in the gift of tongues, especially in the prayer of praise. The Holy Spirit is the Gift that comes into man's heart together with prayer…"who helps us in our weakness" (to pray) (Rom. 8:26). "Therefore, the Holy Spirit not only enables us to pray, but guides us 'from within in prayer…and gives it a Divine dimension'" (cf. Origen, *On Prayer* 2; PG 11:419-423) (*Open the Windows*, p. 51).

27) Spirit baptism gives a deeper insight into the mysteries of God. "No eye has seen, nor ear heard what God has prepared for those who love Him. These things God has revealed to us through the Spirit; for the Spirit searches everything, even the depths of God" (1 Cor.2: 9-10). "We speak of these things in words not taught by human wisdom, but by the Spirit, interpreting spiritual things to those who are spiritual" (1Cor. 2:13).

28) Spirit baptism gives us "discernment of true doctrine" (*Toward a New Pentecost and a New Evangelization*, p. 14). St. John, in an effort to expose false teachers, and give believers assurance of salvation, writes, "I write these things to you concerning those who would deceive you. As for you, the anointing (of the Holy Spirit) you have received from him abides in you, and so you do not need anyone to teach you" (1 John 2:27). "When the Spirit of truth comes, he will guide you into all truth…and he will declare to you all things to come" (John 16:13).

B. Parish/Community Benefits

1) The Spirit-baptized Christian gives witness to and supports the faith-experience of the parish/community that it is the will of God that "all mankind" be baptized into the Holy Spirit. Peter,

in his Pentecost sermon, quoted God's words to the prophet, Joel: "I will pour out my Spirit on all mankind" (Acts 2:17). And Peter added, "the promise is for you, your children and for all who are far away; everyone whom the Lord our God calls to him" (Acts 2:39).

2) There is in the renewal (and in the Spirit-baptized person) a profound sense of the presence of God, which moves those involved toward appreciation of community and a new depth of personal relationships (*Toward a New Pentecost and a New Evangelization,* p. 63). "All who believed were together and had all things in common... day by day they spent time together in the Temple" (Acts 2:44, 46). Spirit baptism gives us the experience of a union with others in a deeper bond of love; a deeper commitment to and a sense of being "part of a building that has the Apostles and the prophets for its foundation" (Eph. 2:20).

3) A parish/community whose members are baptized in the Holy Spirit is empowered to witness to the faith and the need for continuing the same faith-experience and convictions of the early Christians of the infant Church that "the Spirit is not to be quenched..." (1Thess.5:19), but "to fan into flame the Gift (Holy Spirit) of God within by the laying on of hands" (2 Tim. 1:6).

4) The baptism into the Holy Spirit empowers parish/community ministries. A Spirit-baptized parish or community is a "renewed Community of worshippers in a vibrant liturgy, bonded together by the Holy Spirit, serving one another, and committed to an on-going conversion and growth, reaching out to the inactive, the unchurched and the poor. In these parishes or communities, as chronicled in the Acts of the Apostles in the early Church, the charisms (gifts) of the Holy Spirit are identified and welcomed" (*Fanning The Flame,* p. 24).

5) The release of the gifts of the Holy Spirit helps to deepen the faith of the parish and empowers the diverse ministries; what they "see and hear" (1 John 1:3) is the outpouring of the Spirit power that God promised was "to be for all mankind" (Acts

Some Benefits of Receiving the Baptism in the Holy Spirit

2:17); for "everyone whom the Lord our God calls to him" (Acts 2:39). The classical charismatic gifts of the Holy Spirit that Paul mentions in 1 Cor. 12: 8-10 are more readily accepted and "enter into the flow of parish life" (see 1 Cor.14:3,4).

6) Spirit baptism empowers pastoral leaders to witness, to minister and to evangelize. Pastoral leaders "will not only have the vision for a spiritually renewed parish, but the personal experience that will enable them to witness and to minister the life of the baptism into the Holy Spirit to others" (*Fanning The Flame*, p. 24).

7) Persons who are Spirit-baptized better understand and are more open, in a parish or communitarian context, to accept the Scriptural basis for the power of and the uses of the charismatic gifts of the Holy Spirit, including the gift of tongues; and they see that it is God's will that everyone should have this prayer power. The book of Hebrews reads, "He, (Jesus) groaned in the Spirit" (Heb.5:7). St. Paul writes, "Now I would like all of you to speak in tongues" (1 Cor.14:5). Jesus himself referred to this gift: "These signs shall follow those that believe…in my name, they shall speak in new languages" (Mk. 16:17).

8) The Spirit-baptized persons in a parish or community context are more deeply empowered to witness to Christ and the gospel and to make "a bold statement of what the Spirit is saying to the Church." They are strongly aware that "the Spirit is not to be quenched" (1 Thess.5:19).

9) The empowerment of the Spirit has led many to the formation of charismatic prayer groups. The primary purposes of these groups is to manifest their praise of God in prayer and song, scripture sharing, the use of the gifts of the Holy Spirit, witnessing to what the Holy Spirit is doing in their lives, as well as manifesting a "special regard for (and involvement) in the liturgical life of the Church (*Open the Windows*, p. 32). "The appearance of such groups arouses many hopes for the renewal of the whole Church" (p. 4).

C. Benefits in Forwarding Evangelization

1) The Baptism in the Holy Spirit gives the person a deeper awareness of the need for Spirit empowerment for effective evangelization. "A major strength of the renewal is in the area of evangelization. The reestablishment of a personal relationship to Jesus through the experience of the power of the Holy Spirit has made those aware of that power as basis for proclaiming the gospel, arousing faith in others and prompting that faith to unfold and grow in others" (*Toward a New Pentecost and a New Evangelization*,. p. 63). "If there is no Spirit present, there is no evangelization." (*Open the Windows*, p. 19; *Evangelization in the Modern World*).

2) The Spirit-baptized persons, living and acting in their parish, will easily experience and witness to the same Spirit empowerment, faith-experience and convictions of the early Christians, aware that "the Spirit is not to be quenched" (1Thess. 5:19); that it is normal Christian spirituality to be open to "fan into flame the gift of God that is within us by the laying on of my hands" (2Tim. 1:6).

3) "Through Spirit baptism, millions have converted to Christ and committed themselves to service in the Church" (*Fanning The Flame*, p. 13).

4) "This charismatic empowerment (of Spirit baptism) in community in this country and throughout the world...have supplied effective evangelists bringing the gospel...to persons and places otherwise without hope for hearing the good news" (*Fanning The Flame*, p. 13), in bringing others to God or bringing them closer to God.

5) The personal encounter of a parish or community with the person of Jesus, Head of the Church, helps them to be more open and accepting to what the Spirit is saying to the Church. Evangelization, like conversion, is an ongoing process, not a one-time event in the life of the Christian. Because of the personal relationship with Jesus, "we are better prepared for the

Some Benefits of Receiving the Baptism in the Holy Spirit

Spirit-led participation in the Church's mission" (*Fanning The Flame,* p. 23).

6) Spirit baptism empowers and prepares us for "greater participation in the spiritual Body of Christ, the Church. Parishioners are led by the Spirit...for Christian witness accompanied by charism. This evangelization will include verbal witness, examples of life, works of mercy and justice. If a Community is limited in how the Spirit manifests itself (if it "quenches the Spirit"), there is some measure of impoverishment in the total life of the local Church. Suppose an organist has an organ of three keyboards and fifty stops, but plays one keyboard, using ten stops. The full glory of the organ is not exploited; the full richness of the music may not be expressed" (*Toward a New Pentecost and a New Evangelization,* p. 24).

7) The renewal and Spirit baptism encourage authentic ecumenism. Many classical Pentecostals and Protestant neo-Pentecostals share a similar experience (of Spirit baptism). This interplay can offer a sharing of rich spiritual experiences. "Whatever is wrought by the grace of the Holy Spirit in the hearts of our separated brethren can contribute to our own edification" (Vatican II, *Unitatis Redintegratio,* art. 4) (*Toward a New Pentecost and a New Evangelization,* p. 50).

8) The Spirit-baptized Christian is empowered to spread the word and witness to the call of His Holiness Pope Pius VI that the need for a "spiritual renewal" and a "perpetual Pentecost" in the Church is great (*Open the Windows,* pp. 3, 10).

Receiving the Gift of the Holy Spirit

Outline of Program for Receiving the Baptism in the Holy Spirit

Praise and Worship.

Teaching Review (by leader) about the Baptism in the Spirit.

Preparatory Prayer for Receiving the Baptism in the Spirit

    A. Personal Acknowledgement of Our Sinfulness to Jesus

    B. Acknowledging Our Sinfulness to the Community.

    C. Prayer of Repentance.

    D. Turning Away from Sin.

    E. Giving/Asking Forgiveness of God, Ourselves and Others.

    F. Receiving the Redemptive Act of Jesus.

    G. Prayer of Serious Total Commitment to Jesus.

Renewal of Baptismal Promises.

Profession of Faith.

Song of Invocation to The Holy Spirit;

Invocation to Our Blessed Mother, Spouse of the Holy Spirit.

    Prayer for the Baptism in the Holy Spirit before the Laying On of Hands (to give more time in helping each person yield to the gift of praying tongues).

    Laying of Hands on Individuals (if circumstances permit); otherwise, a general invocation for all (see Acts 8:17; 19:6).

Preparatory Prayer for Receiving the Baptism in the Spirit

(Note: In reciting this prayer, omit the scriptural citations, but not the scriptural quotes)

Divine Savior, I come before you in praise, adoration and thanksgiving for your healing love and mercy. I thank you for reminding me of how much you love me by dying on the cross for me and atoning for all my sins. I thank you for always being present for me and hearing my prayer. With the Psalmist I pray, "You have searched me...you know all my thoughts...before a word is on my tongue. . .you know it all" (Ps.139:1-4).

Yet, in your great love, you say, "Come to me, all you who labor and are heavily burdened and I will give you rest" (Matt. 11: 28). Mindful of my human weaknesses, yet with great confidence, I come before you as a helpless child who is in great need of your forgiveness, mercy and healing. Thank you, Lord, for inviting me here so that I could have this heart-to-heart talk with you so that I can be better prepared to receive your great gift of your baptism into the Holy Spirit.

A. Acknowledging Our Sinfulness to Jesus

I am reminded in the words of St. Paul to the Romans that "all have sinned and fall short of the glory of God" (Rom.3:23)...and that "there is no one who is righteous, not even one" (Rom.3: 10). But, Lord, "to whom shall I go? You have the words of eternal life" (John 6:68).

You said, Lord, that "nothing is hidden...that will not come to light" (Luke 8:17). Jesus, you are the Light of the world (John 8: 12); help me to see and take responsibility for all the sins of my life. With that same Light, help me to see any areas of unrepentance and unconfessed or forgotten sin. In a special way, bring to my awareness those sins that have grieved you the most and have kept me separated from you.

In your holy word you say, "Come and pray to me and I will hear you" (Jer. 29: 12). Like the psalmist, I too will be silent before

Outline of Program for Receiving the Baptism in the Holy Spirit

you, Lord (Ps. 37:7), so that being led by your Spirit of Truth, I can more readily acknowledge my sin.

For a short period of silence, listen to the Lord speaking to you interiorly.

With your help, Lord, and like the prodigal son, I acknowledge that I have "sinned against heaven and you" (Luke 15:18), and take responsibility for having "done what is evil in your sight" (Ps.51:4)

B. Acknowledging Our Sinfulness to the Community

In the writings of St. Paul, you remind me that through baptism, we have become "one Body in Christ, with one Lord, one Spirit, one Faith, one God and Father of all" (Eph.4:4-6). "If one member of the Body suffers, then all suffer together with it" (1 Cor.12:26). Help me, Lord, to see how my sinful behavior has hurt you, myself and others by what I have said, done or omitted to do.

The letter of James says, "Confess your sins to one another and pray for one another so that you may be healed" (James 5:18). Help me now, Lord, to acknowledge my sinfulness to you and others so that I may receive your forgiveness and healing.

I confess to Almighty God, and to you, my brothers and sisters, that I have sinned through my own fault, in my thoughts, and in my words, in what I have done and in what I have failed to do. I ask the Blessed Mary, ever Virgin, and all the angels and saints, and you, my brothers and sisters, to pray for me to the Lord, our God.

Sing: Our Father...

C. Prayer of Repentance (Acts 3:19) (Luke 13:3)

Recalling the words of Peter at the first Pentecost, I must "first repent...so that many sins will be forgiven...and then will receive the gift of the Holy Spirit" (Acts 2:38).

Lord, by your Passion, Death and Resurrection, you have atoned for and have taken away all my sins on the condition that I repent and sincerely turn away from sin and anything that leads to sin.

Help me, Lord, to prepare your way into my heart through this "baptism of repentance" (Luke 3:3).

Because you are Love itself, I am truly sorry for all of the sins of my life and for all the times that you were offended by my family and my ancestors. I repent especially of those sins that have grieved you the most and have kept me and them separated from you. With the Psalmist I pray, "Create in me a clean heart, 0 God; put a new and right spirit within me" (Ps.51:10). Mindful of my human weakness, and with your help, Lord, I firmly resolve never to offend you again.

D. Turning Away From Sin (Isaiah 55:7)

You are the same Jesus yesterday, today and forever (Heb.13:8), who loves me with an everlasting love (Jer.31:3). Lord Jesus, your word tells me that you are a merciful and faithful God, and "will not let me be tested beyond my strength...but will provide the way...to endure it" (1 Cor. 10: 13). And you lovingly invite me to come back to you: "Return to me and I will return to you" (Mal. 3:7). Help me, Lord, as I now turn to you and turn away from all wrong doing and avoid everything that leads to sin. From now on I will love, obey, and confess you only as my Lord and Savior (Isaiah 55:7).

Habit of Sin

As it says in the gospel of John, the "born again" person does not have any habit of sin (1 John 3:9). Lord Jesus, bring to my awareness and heal the root cause of any habit of sin in my life. Through the prophet, Isaiah, you tell me that you have come to set me free from the bondage of sin (ls. 61:1).

Release me from any tendency, bondage or enslavement to sin, especially from any addiction to alcohol, drugs, sex, gambling, nicotine and any other addictive habits. Take away all allurement to the sinful ways and standards of the world, the flesh and the devil, so that I no longer find them attractive.

Divine Lord, I want to be free from the dominion of darkness and the rule of Satan. With your help, Jesus, I now renounce any involvement, no matter how small, in any occult activities and in any other powers of darkness.

In the name of Jesus, I now reject and break away from any attractions, allurements, all spiritual bonding to Satanic forces, whether by pacts, vows, dedications, spiritual bonding or any other form of alignment with evil that is contrary to your will and does not give you due honor.

In the name of Jesus, I now reject and dissolve all links and the effects of links with astrologers, mediums, psychics and fortune tellers as well as any activity with ouija boards, tarot cards and any other occult activities.

More than that, Lord, I will destroy and dispose of any books, written pacts, charms, jewelry with Satanic emblems or any other objects that I have that would remind me of or hold me bound to evil forces.

Lord Jesus, I want to be your true follower. You remind me that you are "the Truth and the Life" (John 14:6). So take over my entire life, Lord. Help me to turn to you and the light and the truth of your word that will free me from the enslavement of sin (John 8:34).

E. Prayer for Receiving/Giving Forgiveness

Lord Jesus, your holy word commands us to "put away all anger...to forgive one another as God, in Christ, has forgiven you" (Eph.4:32). Heal the root cause of the hurt in me that sometimes makes it difficult for me to forgive. With all my heart, and with your help, I now let go of any bitterness, anger and unforgiveness that I have toward you, myself and others.

Forgive me, Lord, for becoming bitter and angry with you because I regarded the hard times in my life as punishments from you to me and my family; I know now, that in your eternal wisdom, you sent your only Son, with your healing love that "will never leave me or forsake me" (Heb.13:5); you "discipline me for my good in order that l may share in your holiness" (Heb.12: 10).

Forgiving Others

Your holy gospel reminds me that whenever I stand praying, I should forgive, so that my heavenly Father will forgive me (Mark 11:25). With your Spirit of love, I now forgive and let go of any anger, bitterness or resentment that I have toward anyone, especially toward my parents and other members of my family and relatives, living and deceased, and those persons who have hurt me and my family the most. With your help, Lord, I forgive my ancestors whose transmitted effects of their sins have resulted in my present sufferings and disorders (Lam. 5:7). Forgive the sins of my ancestors, Lord; unbind them from every form of bondage (John 11:44). Replace that bondage with your healing bonds of love (Col. 3:14). Through you, Jesus, I ask them to forgive me for all the times that I have hurt them. Bless them, Lord, and heal all our hurts. Help me to correct my human weaknesses and enable me to understand, love and forgive others.

Forgiving Self

Divine Savior, thank you for helping me to accept and to become more aware of my human weaknesses. Thank you for helping me to forgive all that I think is bad in me. I forgive myself especially for those sins that have hurt you the most and have kept me in spiritual bondage. With your forgiving love, supply what is lacking in my efforts to love and forgive myself and others as you have forgiven.

Lord, I ask you to forgive me also:

1. For the sinful and selfish use of my intellect, my memory, my imagination, my will and my emotions.

    Response: Forgive me and heal me, Jesus.

2. For the sinful and selfish use of my eyes, my ears, my nose, my tongue, my hands and my body.

    Response: Forgive me and heal me, Jesus.

3. For the sinful and selfish use of my spiritual and natural gifts, talents, money, position, time and possessions.

    Response: Forgive me and heal me, Jesus.

4. For the sinful and selfish use of my family, relatives, clergy, friends and other associates.

    Response: Forgive me and heal me, Jesus.

5. For causing others to offend you by the bad example of my

sinful behavior in what I have done or failed to do.

Response: Forgive me and heal me, Jesus.

6. For being resentful and unforgiving toward you or members of my family and relatives, living and deceased, and toward the persons who have hurt me.

Response: Forgive me and heal me, Jesus.

7. For all the times that I was indifferent and did not thank you, or respond to the riches of your graces that you have freely bestowed on me (Eph. 1:6-7).

Response: Forgive me and heal me, Jesus.

8. For the injustice and pain that I have caused my family, relatives and others by my selfish and sinful behavior.

Response: Forgive me and heal me, Jesus.

9. Lord, both I and my "ancestors have sinned...and did not remember the abundance of your steadfast love" (Ps.106: 6-7).

10. For being bitter and unforgiving toward my ancestors whose transmitted effects of their sins and possible involvement with the powers of darkness have resulted in the present sufferings, disorders or wrong inclinations in me or in my family.

Response: Forgive me and heal me, Jesus.

Thank you, Lord, for your great mercy, healing and forgiving love.

F. Receiving the Redemptive Act by Which Jesus Atoned for our Sins

Divine Savior, thank you for reminding me in the gospel of John that as the Father loves you so also you love me (John15:9). How awesome, Lord, is your personal and steadfast love for me! As St. Paul wrote to the Galatians, you "loved me and delivered yourself for me" (Gal.2:20) as if I were the only person in the world. Thank you, Jesus, for dying on the cross for me and atoning for all my sins.

I know that to all who receive you, you give the power to become the children of God (John 1:12). Lord Jesus, I now receive you into my heart, not only as the Redeemer of all mankind, but also as my personal Lord and Savior. By your redeeming act, you atoned for and took upon yourself all of my sins (Rom. 3:24-25; Heb. 2:17). As I place myself under the cross of salvation, pour your redeeming blood over me. Wash and release me from the bondage of sin and erase any feelings of guilt or shame. As you said through your prophet, Isaiah, you "took upon yourself all our sins...as one from whom others hid their faces...despised and held of no account" (Is. 53:3).

G. Prayer of Total Commitment to Jesus as a Born-Again Christian

Thank you, Lord, for reminding me that "every perfect gift is from above, coming down from the Father" (James 1:17), and that you are "the Beginning and the End of all things" (Rev. 1:17).

Thank you, Jesus, for the gift of loving me into being. Thank you for giving to me the life-giving waters of Baptism by which your Holy Spirit came to dwell in me and I became a child of God and a member of your spiritual Body, the Church (Eph. 4:5). By the power of your Holy Spirit, (1 Cor. 12:3) I confess that you, Jesus Christ, are Lord. (Philippians 2:11). All things have been created through you and for you. (Col. 1:16).

Lord Jesus, I want to belong entirely to you. Be Lord of my life. I now unconditionally surrender to you all the areas of my life.

1. Exercise your Divine Lordship over my intellect, my imagination, my memory, my emotions, my will, my spirit, my body and all my natural senses and experiences as well as those of my loved ones.

    Response: Lord, hear my prayer.

2. Be Lord of my family, my business, my money, my plans and my vocation or career in life, as well as that of my loved ones.

    Response: Lord, hear my prayer.

3. Take dominion and be Lord of my past, my present and my future as well as that of all the generations of my family.

Response: Lord, hear my prayer.

4. You are the Lord of the universe. All things came into being through you (John 1:1). Be Lord over all your gifts and possessions that I have now and will have in the future as well as those of my loved ones.

Response: Lord, hear my prayer.

Lord Jesus, by this conversion and "born-again" experience, and my act of total commitment to you, you now become my personal Lord and Savior. For this I thank you and praise you, Lord Jesus.

Renewal of Baptismal Promises (Renunciation of Sin)

1. Do you reject sin so as to live in the freedom of God's children? I do.
2. Do you reject the glamour of evil and refuse to be mastered by sin? I do.
3. Do you reject Satan, father of sin and prince of darkness? I do.
4. Do you reject all his works and all his empty promises? I do.

Profession of Faith

Divine Savior, you tell me in the gospel of John that "God so loved the world that he gave his only Son, so that everyone who believes in him may not perish, but may have eternal life" (John 3:16).

1. Do you believe in God, the Father Almighty, Creator of heaven and earth? I do.
2. Do you believe in Jesus Christ, his only Son, out Lord, who was born of the Virgin Mary, was crucified, died and was buried, rose from the dead and is now seated at the right hand of the Father? I do.
3. Do you believe in the Holy Spirit, the holy Catholic Church, the communion of saints, the forgiveness of sins, the resurrection of the body and life everlasting? I do.

This, Lord, is the faith that I confess, and believe in my heart. I not only believe in the truths that you have revealed to me, but, in a special way, I believe in and accept you as the person of Jesus Christ who is the Son of God and one with the Father and the Holy Spirit.

Song of Invocation to the Holy Spirit.

Invocation to Mary, the Spouse of the Holy Spirit.

Invocation to St. Joseph, Patron of the Interior Life.

Prayer for the Baptism into the Holy Spirit
(Before the Laying On of Hands)

(Note: in reciting this prayer, omit the scriptural citations but not the scriptural quotes)

Lord Jesus, I am reminded in St. Paul's first letter to the Corinthians that I am "a temple of the Holy Spirit" and that God dwells in me (1 Cor.3: 16); and "anyone united to the Lord becomes one spirit with him" (1 Cor. 6: 17).

I want to be "born again," not only of water, but "of water and the Spirit." I want to have the fullness of your Spirit even beyond hat of the "born again" experience (John 3:5).

Mindful of your word, as did your disciples and our Blessed Mother on that first Pentecost, I have placed myself symbolically in the Upper Room, prayerfully preparing for the promise of the Father who you said would "send the Holy Spirit" (Acts 1: 14), I rejoice that the "promise is for everyone... whom the Lord calls to him" (Acts 2:39). Thank you, Lord, for helping me to prepare to become more open and receptive to receive the Father's promise.

You tell me to ask the Father and he will send me the Spirit (Luke 11:13); and that you, Jesus, are the "baptizer into the Holy Spirit" (John 1:33). In your name, Jesus, I now ask the Father to send me the Spirit so that I can experience a new spiritual "rebirth and renewal by your Holy Spirit" (Titus 3:4-6).

Through your prophet Joel you said that you would "pour out your Spirit on all mankind" (Joel 2:28). Pour out your Spirit, Lord.

Outline of Program for Receiving the Baptism in the Holy Spirit

Bring me into that higher level of intimacy of your Spirit's presence and power in me. Bring me into the charismatic dimension of Christian spirituality. As you did to your disciples on that first Pentecost, baptize me and immerse me into the love of the Trinity so that I can experience your divine embrace. Let my Spirit baptism be one that is distinct from and beyond my becoming a Christian through water baptism; even beyond my conversion and "born again" experience.

Lord Jesus, you tell me that "when the Spirit of Truth comes he will guide me into all truth" (John 16: 13); that the Spirit will reveal himself to me (John 14:22) and remind me "of all that you have said" (John 14:25). Help me, Lord, by this personal Pentecost, to become more spiritually sensitive so that I will not only look for the Spirit, but will more readily recognize the Holy Spirit's presence and the work that he wants to do in me. I am confident that you who "have begun a good work in me will bring it to completion" (Phil. 1: 6).

You said in the gospel of John, that you "give the spirit without measure" (John 3:34). Let this Spirit baptism be the beginning of a continuous filling of my intellect, my imagination, my emotions, my will, my memory, my conscience, my spirit and my body, so that being renewed in Spirit, they will always be used according to your will (2 Cor. 5:16-17).

So that I can have a more personal, childlike and intimate relationship with God, my heavenly Father (Gal. 4:6), help me to not only know about you, Lord, but to experience you in my heart as that real person that you are.

Give me a deeper hunger, reverence and understanding of Holy Scripture (Heb. 6:4-5). Help me to understand the importance of obeying the commandments (John 14:21), receiving the sacraments worthily and respecting the authority of the Church (Luke 10:16; John 10:27).

Through personal and community prayer, help me to "grow in the Spirit" (Heb. 10:25), and be fully united with others in the "bonds of peace and love" (Eph. 2:3).

Receiving the Gift of the Holy Spirit

Prayer for the Power from the Spirit

Lord, in the book of Acts you said "you shall receive power when the Holy Spirit comes on you...and you shall be my witnesses... to the ends of the earth" (Acts 1:8). Give me a fresh anointing, Lord, and a fuller release of your Spirit's power and gifts that are already present in me through water baptism and confirmation.

Divine Lord, I do not wish to be just your follower. Take away any indifference that I have toward your Divine Presence in me. Change and release that passive indwelling power of your Spirit in me into that active infilling power. Let that "rose bud" become a "rose bloom," the acorn become the "oak tree," so that I may experience that same infilling power as did the disciples at the first Pentecost.

By that same power, give me a new inner strength over the sinful habits of my life. Help me to become an effective witness for you and draw others to you according to your plan and purpose in my life.

Prayer for the Gifts of the Holy Spirit

Lord, you tell me to "strive for the spiritual gifts, especially that I may prophesy" (1 Cor. 14:1), and that "the Spirit is given without measure" (John 3:34). Strengthen my faith, Lord, so that I can boldly yield to the release of all the spiritual gifts that you want me to experience.

Lord, help me to yield to all the charismatic gifts that you want me to experience, particularly the special gifts that build the faith of the Christian community (1 Cor. 12:8-11). Give me that "entrée gift"—the gift of praying in tongues in a heavenly language which opens the door to the other gifts and is usually a sign that I have been baptized into the Holy Spirit. Make me open to receive any of the other special gifts that you may want to send me: the interpretation of tongues and prophecy; the revelation gifts of word of wisdom, word of knowledge and discernment of spirits; the power gifts of faith, healing and miracle working.

Give me the more important gifts for my personal sanctification: namely, wisdom, understanding, counsel, fortitude, knowledge, piety and reverent fear of the Lord (Isaiah 11:2-3). Fill me,

Outline of Program for Receiving the Baptism in the Holy Spirit

Lord, with the fruit of your Spirit that manifests a deepening of your presence in me and hence are even more important than the gifts of the Spirit: namely, the fruit of love, with its behavioral expressions of joy, peace, patience, kindness, goodness, gentleness, faithfulness and self-control (Gal. 5:22-23). Above all, fill me with a deeper spirit of your love so that my life can be an act of unceasing love and praise.

Lord Jesus, as you are the baptizer into the Holy Spirit, I now ask you to baptize me and immerse me into the heart of the Trinity, so that I can experience the fullness of your divine hug. Help me to yield to the language of the Spirit, the gift of praying in tongues, so that I can praise you in a way that is deeper than my human speech. I ask this, Jesus, in your name. Amen.

This is an appropriate time for the laying on of hands by the prayer group leaders, while encouraging and leading the candidates into the prayer in tongues.

Receiving the Gift of the Holy Spirit

Bibliography

The following references were used as source material in this book.

1. Holy Scripture, *NRSV with Apocrypha.* Zondervan Publishing House. Grand Rapids, MI 49530. c. 1993.
2. Hampsch, John, C.M.F. (audio tape) *The Touch of the Spirit.*
3. Hampsch, John, C.M.F. *What Makes a Person Charismatic?* (Free catalogs for further information on the books, and audio and video tapes and discs by Rev. John Hampsch, C.M.F., may be obtained from: Claretian Tape Ministry, P.O. Box 19100, Los Angeles, California, 90019-0100.)
4. McDonnell, Kilian, and Montague, George T., editors. *Fanning the Flame (What does Baptism in the Holy Spirit Have to Do with Christian Initiation?),* a Michael Glazier Book. The Liturgical Press, Collegeville, Minnesota 56321. Copyright 1991 by the Order of St. Benedict, Inc.
5. McDonnell, Kilian, O.S.B., editor. *Open the Windows (The Popes and the Charismatic Renewal)* Green Lawn Press, 107 South Greenlawn, South Bend, IN 46617. c. 1989.
6. McDonnell, Kilian, O.S.B., editor. *Toward a New Pentecost for a New Evangelization* (*Malines Document* I, second edition), The Liturgical Press, Collegeville, MN 56321. Copyright 1993 by the Order of St. Benedict, Inc.
7. *Catechism of the Catholic Church* 1994. Imprimatur: Joseph Cardinal Ratzinger. 257 W. 17th St., New York, New York, 10011.
8. McCarthy, William J., M.S.A., *Listening to God: Ways to Hearing God's Voice,* My Father's House Retreat Center, P.O. Box 22, Moodus, Connecticut 06469. (860) 873-1581. Reproduced with permission from: *St. Joseph Baltimore Catechism #1.* Catholic Book Publishing Company. New York, NY, c. 1964.

9. Donahue, Rev. Terry C.C., Companions of the Cross, *The Gift of Tongues in the Liturgy of the Early Church* (4/11/97). Ottawa, Ontario, Canada.

10. Father Gabriel of Saint Mary Magdalene, O.C.D., *Divine Intimacy (Meditation on the Interior Life for Every Day)*, TAN Publishers, Inc. Rockford, IL 61105.

11. Kelsey, Martin T., *"Tongue Speaking: An Experiment in Spiritual Experience."* Hodder and Stoughton. Toronto. c. 1968. (Taken from: *The Gift of Tongues in The Liturgy*, by Rev. Terry Donahue, C.C.).

12. Recommended reading: *"Then Peter Stood Up..."* International Catholic Charismatic Renewal Services. Rome, Italy. (A collection of the Popes' Addresses to the Catholic Charismatic Renewal from its Origin to the year 2000; a supplement extends this to the year 2002.)

This material may not be reproduced to be sold, but may, without further permission, be reproduced to serve the Body of Christ. Free catalogs are available on this and other spiritual materials by Father John Hampsch, C.M.F., from the Claretian Tape Ministry, P.O. Box, 19100, Los Angeles, California 90019-0100. Phone: (323) 734-1234. Web site: www.claretiantapeministry.org